Funeral Festivals in America

DISCARD

Material Worlds
Simon J. Bronner, Series Editor

*Designing the Centennial: A History of the 1876
International Exhibition in Philadelphia*
by Bruno Giberti

Culinary Tourism
edited by Lucy M. Long

Funeral Festivals in America

Rituals for the Living

Jacqueline S. Thursby

THE UNIVERSITY PRESS OF KENTUCKY

Publication of this volume was made possible in part by
a grant from the National Endowment for the Humanities.

Editorial and Sales Offices: The University Press of Kentucky
663 South Limestone Street, Lexington, Kentucky 40508-4008
www.kentuckypress.com

Cataloging-in-Publication Data is available from
the Library of Congress.

ISBN 978-0-8131-9299-4 (pbk: acid-free paper)

This book is printed on acid-free recycled paper meeting
the requirements of the American National Standard
for Permanence in Paper for Printed Library Materials.

Manufactured in the United States of America.

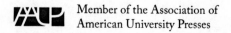

Member of the Association of
American University Presses

To Grace, Ruth, and Helen
for your friendship in life and dignity in death.

"And Tom brought him chicken soup until he wanted to kill him. The lore has not died out of the world, and you will still find people who believe that soup will cure any hurt or illness and is no bad thing to have for the funeral either."

John Steinbeck, *East of Eden*

Contents

Acknowledgments

Many colleagues, friends, and generous family members have shared their experiences and suggestions for this text. First, Simon Bronner, folklorist, has answered questions and has provided consistent support during the daunting textual construction and reconstruction of the work. From its original categorical arrangement to its present thematic format, he, and Joyce Harrison, editor, have encouraged me. Lauren Gillespie, my able research assistant, and Anthony Dunster, a Brigham Young University computer-lab guru, helped me to accomplish the task in a timely manner. Last, my husband, Denny, has served as friend, valuable critic, and one of those stalwart friends "who only stand and wait," for the last few years while I have worked. Thank you all.

Prologue

Contemporary American funerals often assume the character and roles of festival. That presents a paradox in conflict with traditional perceptions of ritual behaviors associated with death. Human beings characteristically invent and reinvent traditional folklife to suit their contemporary needs. With changes over time in cultural attitudes and behaviors, familiar traditional customs become intertwined with newly discovered or created practices, and new modes emerge.[1] The American character commonly adapts old ways to new, and the United States, a complex civilization made up of its own indigenous people and multitudes of cultures from around the world, has reinvented the response to death. Rather than a space of time with emphasis on separation, death and the funerary rituals surrounding it have become a place for renewal and reaffirmed connectedness between family and friends of the deceased.

Research using the folkloristic[2] lens loans itself to synthesizing material from various academic disciplines. Examining oral, material, customary, and belief systems as applied to both traditional and newly invented funerary ritual opens to examination a broad range of cultural responses. Ritual practices discussed range from clothing to foods to epitaphs. To illuminate the subject of contemporary American funerary rituals and practices, I have selected some comparative examples to draw out the variety of cultural responses (both folk and commercial) using America as a laboratory for diversity and at the same time, standardization.

The following discussion represents both my objective and subjective perspectives because I have loved, celebrated, and accepted the passing of many beautiful lives; I have mourned, reflected, and come to understand how tenuous and fleeting life is in spite of the sense of invulnerability most of us seem to have.

When Evelyn Waugh wrote *The Loved One* (1948) as a satire of the elaborate preparations and memorialization of the dead taking place in his time, he had no way of knowing how extraordinarily creative and technical human funerary practice would become. Human remains and cremains are now commonly scattered, buried simply or elaborately, preserved in methods that may be as complex (or more so) than the ancient Egyptian mummification techniques, or even launched into orbit. In my personal experience, I have not seen "a chintz sofa . . . [with] what seemed to be the wax effigy of an elderly woman dressed as though for an evening party" (Waugh 1999: 49), but I have seen Web sites with videos and pictures of the deceased, tombstones and crypts with embedded tape recordings of music, and pneumatically etched portraits on cemetery markers so lifelike that one might imagine that the replicated eyes are following the viewer's movement. Waugh would have enjoyed *The Young and the Dead*, an HBO film about the Hollywood Forever Cemetery, which tells the story of what owner and director Tyler Cassidy has done with this cemetery to revive and restore dignity, memory, and connectedness in the ongoing relationship between bereaved survivors and deceased loved ones.

Grave sites from antiquity give evidence of the general human belief in survival after death. It is commonly known that Egyptian and Chinese (and other) tombs contained artifacts, including foods, to assist the dead in the afterworld. Fossilized imprints throughout the world, from Turkey to South America, have enabled anthropologists and other scholars to discern that the ancient dead were buried with flowers, indicating that death may have been perceived as a celebratory occasion. Both ancient and contemporary belief systems teach followers of a form of life beyond the grave, and there are always stories circulating about near-death experiences or even spirits who return with occasional messages. How the dead are treated is a hallmark of civilization, and for eons, evidence suggests that they were usually treated with some measure of honor and respect.

My folkloric and cultural research situates this contemporary mourning, funerary, and food study in the realm of celebration and festival, and it will present further evidence for that placement. My research has included wide participant observation. Much of the following discussion and interpretation is consequent to my personal interaction with various religious denominations practiced in the United States. I also taught "Religions in America" at Bowling Green State University, and I have attended Latter-day Saint, Protestant, Roman Catholic, Greek Orthodox, Jewish, Buddhist, and Hindu religious services and funerals. In each of those settings, I have been warmly welcomed, and though I have asked many questions and was given materials to read, I have been constantly honored by being invited to return. Feasting and the ubiquitous presence and importance of food in relation to death and mourning convince me that ritual funeral behaviors are folk expressions for the living. It is difficult, if not impossible, to enjoy a good meal and company when one is sad, and post-funeral meals, usually sumptuous and comforting, are no exception. The great critic and scholar Mikhail Bakhtin stated that "Sadness and food are incompatible. . . . The banquet always celebrates a victory and this is part of its very nature."[3] The funerary banquet celebrates a life, often well lived, and the victory is in overcoming and accepting the change that death brings; honoring a loved one at death becomes victorious because it renews the living.

This study also reveals diminished boundaries that the acknowledgment and celebration of death create between varied members of our social, cultural, and ethnic strata. There are pinnacle moments of harmony that occur when common human emotion responds with wisdom and dignity to meaningful, tender, and life-impacting rites of passage. Arnold van Gennep, Victor Turner, Jacques Derrida, and Peter Narváez and others have furnished our scholarship with sensitive and profound insights concerning death and belief. In this discussion of American life and its response to death, we will see that Americans question, mourn, and then celebrate with ongoing, forward-looking confidence in the continued joy of life. We live in a different time now than when some of these scholars conducted their research and coined their theories. We live in a world connected by technology and diminished in vastness to what Marshall McLuhan called a global-sized village.[4] With this diminished sense of distance has come a positive empathy unlike the world has known before. With that empathy has come the recognition that the living need the living. We are linked through knowledge of one another's triumphs and tragedies, and we are responding to one another globally.

Americans respond to myriad rites of passage between birth and death, the inevitable bookends of mortality. And for most of us, ritual behaviors are often festive celebrations of life in process, transitions and transformations, even at the time of death. The bereaved need to find a balance between restorative solitude, continued social interaction—*communitas*, and validation at the time of a death. That can easily challenge a sense of appropriateness. Each person affected must find a balance between personal response and public demeanor under strained and socially dictated circumstances. The question is about how to locate the congruous behaviors and relationships within these various events and circumstances. Victor Turner reminded us of how difficult it is to find appropriate relationships between conflicts of time and place, between traditional behavior and community expectations,[5] yet that space must be found and allowed.

We seek what Turner calls a "transformative experience" with others that reaches deeply into the "root" of our being and "finds in that root something profoundly communal and shared" (Turner 1969: 138). It is in that seeking that we reach out to others to both give and receive comfort in times of crisis. Appropriateness, in an age of permissiveness and sanctioned spontaneity, is a slippery concept that conflicts with many culturally bound constructions. But our society and culture are maturing, and Americans are finding adaptive balance and appropriate response in the midst of our dynamic and amorphous culture. The consequence of this boundary crossing is increased understanding of those who may be very different culturally and socially from ourselves, and that is good. It is moral, and ethical, and it helps bring to mind Derrida's reflection about what do I love when I love my

God? The "God" doesn't matter; it is about what and how we can love one another when we love our God (Caputo 1997: 9).

Our legacies include influences and practices carried over from the Ancient World. Long ago, Homer described funerary rites in *The Iliad* that were carried out as a solemn and vital part of military practice. It was an insult to human life for a corpse to be left in a battlefield where it might be consumed by sun, stray animals, and insects. To construct a funeral pyre for cremation of the body was a serious responsibility, and there were mourning rites that were to be observed. When Patroklos was killed, dressed for death, and then placed on the crematory pyre, Achilles stated that he will "heap a mound over him," and "cut my hair for him." These acts, described in Book Twenty-three of Homer's *Iliad*, are ritual demonstrations by the living in honor of the dead person's station and prestige. The flames were lit, burned a while, and were eventually extinguished with wine. The collected bones were placed in a jar for future burial, ideally, in their homeland. After the cremation, particularly if the deceased was important, there were funeral games and competitions and among the prizes were valuable possessions of the deceased. The games were followed by a huge banquet:

> Aiakides, who set the funeral feast in abundance
> before them; and many shining oxen were slaughtered with the stroke
> of the iron, and many sheep and bleating goats and numerous
> swine with shining teeth and the fat abundant upon them
> were singed and stretched out across the flame of Hephaistos,
> The blood ran and was caught in cups all around the dead man.
> (Homer [trans. by Richmond Lattimore] 1961: 451)

Such elaborate preparations for the funeral feast are generally no longer practiced (we have restaurants and caterers today), but the concept of the mourners' meal has continued. We gather together and look back; we eat, laugh, and then together look forward to joy and success in the future.

In the introduction to *Of Corpse: Death and Humor in Folklore and Popular Culture*, Peter Narváez wrote that Americans laugh at the juxtapositions of death and humor in today's world, and this understanding of the unpredictable and incongruous realities helps us cope.[6] Americans have always managed to keep a sense of humor even in the grimmest circumstances. Though this is not a text about humor as a concept, it *is* a text about good humor. It is a narrative about the joy and solace present in living human behavior—sometimes an almost ironic presence when the final curtain is closed on someone's life. Traditional rituals and associated behaviors recognize and celebrate the ongoing nature of human life, and the perception of that ongoing life ranges from living in memory to living literally in another dimension. Those rites validate and construct the deeply important play of festivals and celebrations even at the time of death.

Of course, death is a finality, a closure, a material end. It harbors suffering, separation, and sorrow for the survivors and for the one who has met death after a prolonged illness. Sudden death, a staggering blow, conveys both shock *and* sorrow. Caring bystanders are compelled to reach out to those whose lives have been altered by the change. Again turning to an early example in *The Iliad*, Achilles, upon hearing of the death of his dear friend Patroklos:

> caught up the grimy dust, and poured it
> over his head and face, and fouled his handsome countenance,
> and the black ashes were scattered over his immortal tunic.
> And he himself, mightily in his might, in the dust lay
> at length, and took and tore at his hair with his hands, and
>   defiled it. . . .
> On the other side Antilochos mourned with him, letting the tears fall,
> and held the hands of Achilleus as he grieved in his proud heart,
> fearing Achilleus might cut his throat with the iron.
> (Homer [trans. by Richmond Lattimore] 1961: 375–76)

People must be protected and consoled at the time of loss. During the mourning period both preceding and following a funeral or memorial service, great varieties of comforting foods and warm gatherings are a part of the familiar and traditional process. The burial or cremation in most American cultures is followed with a celebratory meal where friends and loved ones gather in joy-filled reunion, and the emphasis, through nourishing foods and warm validation, is placed on life and ongoing relationships rather than closure.

This discussion about life, ritual, and paradox in America's death tradition focuses on celebratory and festive moments in human behavior that illuminate endeavors to create instances of diminished social stratifications. For a climactic moment at a christening or infant naming, wedding, *bar* or *bat mitzvah,* baptism, or death ceremony, the participants and the audience become one in understanding and purpose. Those high, ritualistic points in time are to be celebrated because, for an instant, everyone present is in harmony. At that modicum of time, neither history, age, wealth, nor community stature matter, and communion occurs within the assembly. The moment is soon broken by movement and gentle smiles, but an enigma intervenes because some sacrosanct restraint deep in our archetypal psyche dictates solemnity at such high communal moments. We forbid demonstrative shouts of joy during that sacred pinnacle, but shortly afterward a banquet is spread, the participants relax, and the joy of human interaction and pleasure begins once again.

Ritual behaviors at the time of serious illness and subsequent death of a beloved friend or family member, or a known and valued member of the community, have occurred throughout the history of the human family. Mourning is work; it is a solemn period of adjustment to absence and change. Grief for the transition of a valued person and the continued solemnity of the bereaved over days or even weeks builds psychological pressure within the dispossessed. From Sigmund Freud to Elizabeth Kübler-Ross, psychologists and scholars have searched for understanding of the grieving personality. Because of the common recognition that the bereaved may become emotionally or psychologically disabled without a restoration of normalcy in the permanent absence of the deceased, friends and family members extend support and comfort in a variety of ways. For most bereaved, the healing process begins soon after the death. Over time one learns to accept the absence of the loved one and is able to leave the heaviness of heart behind. Even so, healing is often slow, and unfortunately for some, healing is never complete.

Even so, life goes on, and in the culture of the United States, support and comfort at the time of the death, and sometimes for an extended period after the death, is often in the form of celebration. That the gatherings even become festive is a reality well recognized in our society. The celebrations have even been commodified (foods, decorations, and mementos for funeral banquets of nearly every culture in the United States are easily ordered on the Internet).

The multitalented actor, director, and writer Woody Allen once remarked, "My grandfather had a wonderful funeral. . . . It was held in a big hall with accordion players. On the buffet table there was a replica of the deceased in potato salad" (Allen 2002: n.p.). Colonial settlers in the United States continued European traditions in which food played an important role in relation to funerary ritual and celebration. From foodstuffs being left at the grave site at regular intervals, sometimes over the span of many years, to funeral potatoes (a cheese and potato casserole) commonly used at post-funeral dinners from the Midwest to Utah, food as a giver and sustainer of life has been a symbolic part of the festive ritual behavior of mourning and funerary tradition. For a post-funeral dinner to metamorphose into a reunion party of sorts is more common than uncommon. People live and love and celebrate their very being.

Recently, my husband's oldest aunt died. She was a clear-headed ninety-three-year-old and preplanned her open-casket funeral with directions that her body was to be cremated after the service. Her ashes were to be buried in a local cemetery, and she had already designed and paid for her granite headstone. The viewing period (about four hours) was enhanced by a video panorama of photographs representing her life from infancy to grandmother. After the funeral, which was a sober memorial and tribute by close relatives and associates, her directions were for family and friends to go to an Italian restaurant on the "hill" in St. Louis for a dinner in her honor. She had funded it, it was an open menu, and about thirty people (including grandchildren) attended. There the occasion became festive and celebratory. Obviously a thoughtful and generous woman, Aunt Virginia wanted to be remembered as one who had lived a successful life of joy and service. Feeding people (particularly Thanksgiving dinners) had been an important part of her life, and in today's accepting culture, she was able to design her funeral and arrange a closure that represented what she personally valued.

The funerary celebration just described was for an elderly Protestant woman. Similar manifestations of grief, soberness, and tenderness are present in all groups, and food is commonly offered as a consolation and comfort to those who, for a while, may be disconsolate. After the burial, for most if not all groups, there is a meal. Prepared and served by caterers, volunteers, or a restaurant, the reunion of family and friends gathered in honor of the deceased is social and communal. The food is plentiful, and at that point the reality of a transition for the deceased and the continuity of life for the living has become a stronger affect. The grief and mourning is not over, but that meal provides sustenance and a place for shared memories, reunion, and joy. Americans like to celebrate, and the funeral experience, as somber as the cause may be, has moments of festivity that touch every cultural family in the contemporary United States of America.

The connections made at those post-funeral dinners, or even banquets, suggest to me that a revision in Arnold van Gennep's classic organization of the structure of the rites of passage is in order. Rather than separation, transition, and incorporation, I suggest that in funerary ritual, the focus is on the process of the funeral celebration itself. Rather than van Gennep's triadic process, I would suggest a more fitting contemporary rite of passage would be described as *awakening, transmutation,* and *connectedness*—a contemporary metamorphosis that will be explicated more fully in chapter 2.

We live in a largely secular world. Though many Americans belong to a church and even attend congregational services or Mass regularly, conflicts between the generations occur because the older generation often adheres to traditional customs, and the younger generation sometimes finds that practice irrelevant to its own lived experience. At the time of death, many Americans, both young and old, are learning to be flexible about standardized procedures. Longstanding traditional approaches emphasizing religious and community functions are giving way to invented or individualized rituals. These

newly invented folkways provide meaning for both individuals and
the immediate family and friends.

Though this discussion is focused more on the living than the
dead and more on unity than divisiveness, it represents individual interpretation. Americans, in their plurality, are both different and
alike, but at the time of sorrow, or calamity, or of a private or public
death, they tread common ground. Death hurts, but all of our cultures have found ways to soothe that distress and press on. This may
sound like a sweeping generality, but I believe that the normative
American view of death includes a certain pragmatic sense of invulnerability. Americans, no matter their country of origin, seem to
accept death as the occasional price of continued freedom. That acceptance, as painful as it may be on an individual basis, yields a
brave, practical victory over death. Looking back a moment at American history, we recall the nationalistic, patriotic, and independent
spirit of this country. I suggest that vital spirit is still alive and well in
the United States. Centuries ago we threw off British control, then
slavery and other threats of oppression. For better or for worse,
Americans continue to defy inappropriate aggression both at home
and around the world. Both collectively and individually, Americans
generally seem to deny death as a deterrent to our national goals. Unlike some cultures present in the United States that embrace the "eternal self" and the cycle of *Samsára*, or reincarnation, the majority of
Americans embrace life, this mortal life, both as individuals and as a
national collective. Most Americans, both individually and collectively, believe in one life as well-lived as possible.

With engaging compassion, Americans watch or read the death
statistics of our military personnel serving in harm's way and mourn
with the families when an irreplaceable human life is lost in defense
of our freedom. We watch and pray with anxiety when a ship is cap-
sized, when miners are trapped beneath the earth, when a plane is
hijacked, or when a child is kidnapped. We are a nation that clearly
values individual life, and we suffer in an almost childlike manner,
spontaneously and visually, when life is lost. We rally together in disaster, and we celebrate together in victory. But for most Americans,
even this shared passion to know the statistics so as to grasp the real-

ity or size of an event, and pray for the suffering becomes quickly distant and even a little surreal. There seemed to be little lasting, deep collective engagement with disaster and tragedy until September 11, 2001. Further, our nation's response to the destruction and apparent hundreds of thousands of deaths caused by the December 2004 tsunami reveals the deeply linked empathy and compassion Americans share with the world community.

Prior to these disasters, most Americans were comfortable with a fix-it mentality—a concept that death didn't need to be a part of their lived reality. It was there, but it was given little appreciation or afterthought. The events of both of those tragic events have sent a ripple of sobering reality through the nation, and our people became aware that America was not untouchable after all, and that technology could not defeat or control natural disaster. In a society that values life so much, an evolving, dynamic society made up of cultures from around the world, the startling reality of thousands of funerals and memorial services, mass burials, and cremations performed in a brief span of time, was a trigger for deep emotional response and an understanding of the fragile nature of life itself. These events reminded the nation of the importance of sacrifice, the central importance of family when it comes to the line between life and death, and the deep meaning of nationalism and kinship across socioeconomic, cultural, and ethnic boundaries.

Personal responses of survivors of these tragedies are countless, and most Americans seem to know at least one person whose life was directly impacted by these tragic disasters. In discussing lived, human performance, we are deconstructing often unself-conscious behaviors representing honest and emotional responses to the reality of life and death. We responded to the tragedy of September 11, 2001, with the deepest horror and grief. On the other hand, it wasn't long before urban lore, sick jokes, and mythic miracle stories arose almost literally from the ashes. Restoring eating places and normal mercantile culture in the area was a priority. A few months ago I visited Soho, a shopping district near where the towers were, and in that eclectic bustle of American energy, merchandise ranged from Twin Tower T-shirts to World Trade Center chocolates. Americans, generally optimistic by heritage and inclination, steadied themselves once again, and have moved forward with a renewed sense of pride and, again, that sense of American invulnerability in spite of continuing tragedies of hurricanes, earthquakes, and erupting volcanoes. Much of the Asian world, impacted beyond the scope of belief or understanding by the death-dealing tsunami, will need support from the world community for generations to come. Accounts of miracles and even ghost stories have emerged from the tragedy, and there will be thousands more ahead. The human spirit moves on in life in spite of loss and death.

In the course of human experience, death has been an intrusive reality surrounded with countless cultural constructions. Ideas, beliefs, and ritual practices have become reified with time and practice, and in today's experimental climate, supposed reifications are often challenged. Ancient beliefs and customs are reinterpreted and reinvented to suit contemporary points of view. In order to assist human negotiation with the shock and emotional chaos that death often visits upon the survivors, ritual practices—including funerary systems, mourning rituals, and familiar, associated foods—help to restore normalcy, pattern, and balance. For contemporary Americans, the elements of the rite of passage can appropriately be described as awakening or vivification (arriving at accountability), transmutation (a dynamic process of change), and connectedness (becoming part of a synergistic web). As we mature, awaken, and become sensitive to the world around us, we move into a web of give-and-take relationships. The funerary process, with its myriad rituals and constructions, aids humans in strengthening that living web of intra- and interpersonal relationships.

The paradox that touches upon the celebratory nature of most American funerals occurs because of the very ambiguity of human nature. Though it is a time of separation and transition for the deceased, it is a time of tribute and ritual festival for the survivors. With increasing acceptance of personal individuality in the manner in which a funeral or memorial service is conducted, many funeral tributes become occasions of joy, rather than sadness. In America, the joy of human interaction and celebration can take place even while an individual is dying. In some cultures, Hindu for instance, it is not uncommon for the elderly to separate themselves from family activities and seek solitude to prepare for the transition of death. In the United States, though, most of the elderly, whether at home or in professional care centers, are included in the stir of social interaction as long as possible.

Some years ago, the late anthropologist Barbara Myerhoff gave us a beautiful story about an elderly gentleman, Jacob Koved, who died in a senior citizens' center at the celebration of his ninety-fifth birthday party. Part of Jacob's legacy was a financial donation that provided for five more birthday parties "whether he was there or not" (Myerhoff 1980: 200). His donation was to provide for celebrations and to raise money for Israel. At Jacob's death, the family directed the onlookers to continue the party, and they did.

To celebrate across boundaries and with one another is also an American way, and the irony of joy, in spite of mourning, surrounds our response to death. In an increasingly multicultural public sphere, our nation at last seems to be learning respect for one another's ongoing (and treasured) differences as education has improved and reached more people. Beyond the exotic, beyond curiosity, we are a nation learning to live together in peace and communitas. Could it be, in part, media programming, children's programs like Mr. Rogers' Neighborhood or Sesame Street, that has inspired a legacy of acceptance of one another's differences? We have two generations who have grown up with those shows, and among them are today's caregiving professionals: pastors, bishops, psychologists, counselors, and funeral directors. One can wonder about the catalysts for genuine tolerance for differences among us. Was it the Civil Rights Movement, Rosa Parks, Martin Luther King Jr., Lyndon B. Johnson, and the Kennedys? In our society today, first and fourteenth generations of Americans work together, share their cultures, and attend funerary celebrations across ethnic and religious boundaries of the past.

In previous centuries, death was a constant presence in both the community and the family circle, and children were familiar with the event. Today, though, I think it safe to say that most contemporary American children have little knowledge of death—despite the fact that in some countries of the world death is certainly no stranger to children. There have been times in the United States, however, when death has not been remote or obscure to children. In Southern Utah, for instance, radiation poisoning became so common for a period of time that "Downwinders," adults who were children during that period of frequent radioactive fallout from bomb tests, recall that even as children they realized they would probably die prematurely of cancer. Preston Truman, an individual who later went on to found the Downwinders Organization, stated: "I remember in school they showed a film once called *A is for Atom: B is for Bomb*. I think most of us who grew up in that period, we've all in our own minds added 'C is for Cancer, D is for death'" (Fox 2005: qtd. from Gallagher 1993: 315).

In the United States, the dying, in their last stages, and the dead are usually removed promptly from the family circle. If there is a common viewing followed by a typical, American funeral, children are often left out. That is not always true, but it is a frequent practice. Our American children view play-acted death constantly, in the popular media, but it is abstract, unemotional, and does not seem to have much impact on most of them. If there is a death in the immediate family of a sibling or primary caregiver, children in our society often benefit from professional counseling. Most families are not prepared to assist children with these kinds of realities; it is a situation not unlike the counseling necessary for children and teens when unexpected tragedy, like a school bus accident or deadly school explosion or attack, happens to strike their school or community.

Folkloric research as well as other academic disciplines situate American funerary practices, including wakes, eulogies, banquets, and cemetery lore, in the realm of festival and even humor, and the public interest in these topics is strong. *Of Corpse: Death and Humor in Folklore and Popular Culture* (2003), edited by Peter Narváez, provides essays that range from disaster jokes and rites of passage to festivals and popular narratives. *One Foot in the Grave: The Strange But True Adventures of a Cemetery Sexton* (2001) by Chad Daybell, introduces us to grandmas who steal decorations, graveside lovers, and lock-picking ghosts. *Death Warmed Over: Funeral Food, Rituals, and Customs from around the World* (2004) by Lisa Rogak, is, as the flyleaf states: "A unique cookbook that shows you how to incorporate long-standing cultural traditions—from the Amish and Eskimo to Greek and Polish—into the planning of a well-rounded celebration of life." *Multicultural Celebrations: Today's Rules of Etiquette for Life's Special Occasions* (1999) by Norine Dresser, informs us of proper responses to occasions, including funerals, in those cultures with which we may not be familiar. From *Cemetery Stories: Haunted Graveyards, Embalming Secrets, and the Life of a Corpse after Death* (2001) by Katherine Ramsland, and *Giving Voice to Sorrow: Personal Responses to Death and Mourning* (2001) by Steve Zeitlin and Ilana Harlow, to Jacques Derrida's *The Gift of Death* (1995) and *The Work of Mourning* (2001), texts and television shows (*Crossing Over* and *Six Feet Under)* reflect an interest in death and related topics.

Not only is public interest in the discussion and response to death strong, commercial interest in public curiosity and concern is also thriving. Prepaid burial plans are ubiquitous, and interested customers may even buy their own caskets at two of the Wal-Marts in Chicago. Though I haven't seen those caskets, I understand that they are in the back of the stores by the mattresses, and can be bought for about eight hundred dollars each. As an added note of history, purchasing a casket from a furniture store was a common practice in the nineteenth century. If you can find a photograph of a furniture store from 1860–1900, you might see coffins standing upright at the rear of the store. They were available for purchase just like any other home furnishing.

Classic dictionary, folkloristic, and anthropological definitions of celebrations and festivals provide primary evidence for the supposition that funerals are celebrations. The meaning of the word celebrate, as listed in *Webster's New World Dictionary,* is: "1) to perform (a ritual, ceremony, etc.) publicly and formally: solemnize; 2) to commemorate . . . with ceremony or festivity; 3) to honor or praise publicly; 4) to mark (a happy occasion) by engaging in some pleasurable activity" (235). The late Richard Dorson, folklorist and scholar, suggested that "the term *celebration* can encompass festivals, rituals, ceremonies, spectacles, pageants, fetes, holidays, and partakes of all these elements" (Dorson 23 qtd. in Turner's *Celebration*). Victor Turner, a leading American folklorist and mythologist, wrote that society is essentially a work in process, and "The word *celebration* is derived from the Latin *celeber*, 'numerous and much frequented,' and relates to the vivacity—akin to what the great French sociologist Emile Durkheim called 'effervescence'—generated by a crowd of people with shared purposes and common values" (Turner 1982: 16).

Celebrations often mark rites of passage by providing a framework in which groups can perform certain traditional customs and behaviors. Birth, baptism, circumcision, puberty, marriage, initiation into certain groups, and funeral define our mortal journey. Ceremonial variants, according to cultural tradition and invention, unbind routine and day-to-day social structures, and the celebration provides a sense of communal connectedness. Celebration provides a time to be together in a specific space for a determined time. It is a safe pocket of retreat in which participants can move from serious cultural obligation to lighter social interplay.

Festival is a *cultural performance*. The same dictionary quoted above defines festival as: "1) a time of day of feasting or celebration; esp., a periodic religious celebration; 2) a celebration, entertainment, or series of performances of a certain kind, often held periodically . . . ; 3) merrymaking; festivity" (*Webster's* 2002: 524). Anthropologist/folklorist Alessandro Falassi's writes in *Time Out of Time: Essays on the Festival* that "the term *festival* derives ultimately from the Latin *festum*. But originally Latin had two terms for festive events: *festum*, for 'public joy, merriment, revelry,' and *feria*, meaning 'abstinence from work in honor of the gods'" (Falassi 1987: 2). Scholars from the disciplines of comparative religion, anthropology, sociology, and folklore have examined festivals from various perspectives over time. Collecting, categorizing, analyzing, and describing or discussing is the work of these social scientists, and festival has been an interest and concern of scholars for centuries. Questions about the survival of ancient patterns and folk customs continue to be explored, analyzed, and reinterpreted. A festival is a time set aside for celebration. Festivals in the late twentieth century can be traced to earlier practices in the United States, and "at the most basic level, there are homegrown, grassroots festivals organized by and for a particular community."[7] I suggest that the funeral ritual in the United States has become just that. A yearly assemblage in a park, as practiced by a family in Utah, is to read poetry and sing in honor of the deceased, release balloons, and then follow with a picnic and games for the children. That annual behavior seems to meet Brunvand's criteria for ceremony, which is a celebration of "true folk customs . . . especially those that require 'rights of passage'—birth and adolescence, coming of age, courtship and marriage, and death" (Brunvand 1998: 408).

A funeral is a *cultural performance*. Funeral rituals move people into a period of paradox and irony because of culturally carried misconceptions of the mourning period and funerary behaviors. In the reality of practice, it is often a gathering, a renewal, a rebirth of a sort, of relationships and connections. The rites of passage we call "funerary" meet the defining criteria for both celebration and festival. It is an occasion of "crowds of people" and "for a particular community." It is only in part a solemn, ritualistic, ceremonial performance. Though it is not always public or formal, it can be both. It is a commemoration, and its atmosphere is often one of pleasurable activity. At the wake, or viewing, there is often a vivacity, a sense of ongoing life, and "a crowd of people with shared purposes and common values." As festival, the funeral, mourning, and foods are all *cultural performances*. Though it may not be regular "periodic religious celebration," it occurs periodically in all cultures. For most funerary practice, the second Latin definition is appropriate: "*festum* is abstinence from work in honor of the gods." Funeral rituals follow ancient patterns and folk customs; it is a time for the *celebration* of a life, and it is "organized by and for a particular community."

In our fast-paced American world, we easily overlook plans for the disruption that death of a relative or close friend means to routine, everyday life. Ritual responses to the change, usually formulaic according to the belief system or cultural practices followed, provide a steadying window of adjustment. It is difficult to clearly comprehend that someone deeply cared about, a presence in our life, will be permanently gone from our association. Consequently, it has become natural for most humans to think of death more in terms of transition than separation, and varied belief systems further elaborate that perception with diverse cultural constructions. In Arnold van Gennep's classic text, *The Rites of Passage,* he reminds us that though an observer might expect "rites of separation" to be most prominent, the reality he observed was the emphasis on transition from this world in incorporation into the next.[8] And yet, I realized as I have researched, observed, and gathered records of myriad mourning, funeral, and memorial practices, that the contemporary emphasis was less on the separation and transition of the deceased and more on the bonding or even binding of the surviving family and friends. There are elaborate rites in some cultures that "incorporate the deceased into the world of the dead," but phone calls and e-mails notify and invite the living, extended family for the gathering. And with the explanations and arrangements come inquiring questions about one another's well-being and about one another's lives and families.

It is a time of transition and change for both the living and the deceased, and the "correct" procedures of the deceased's belief system are explored and sometimes tailored to meet the planners' needs, but there is more than that. Various proscribed religious dietary requirements are taken into consideration, and the funeral or memorial service subsequently planned can range from turning the responsibility over to a commercial undertaking establishment to the personalized and contemporary practice of "green burial" (mostly do-it-yourself burial in a natural setting—not always a cemetery). There are many creative layers of interpretation and styles in-between. All along the way, however, as I talked to people and read about funerary customs, I observed a togetherness—a working together and liveliness of the families. The conversation was often an exchange and consensus about how best to "celebrate" the deceased's life, and of course, how to participate appropriately in the celebration. In sum, I observed the separation and transition of the deceased to result in behaviors more about the living and less about the dead.

American Funerary Practice in the Seventeenth and Eighteenth Centuries

Long before Europeans came to establish permanent settlements in the Americas, Native Americans, both hunters and planters, lived in coastal and inland areas, as well as arctic and tropical environments. These vast continents were inhabited by ancient tribes with long established cultural and ritual behaviors. Concrete discoveries, conjectures, and theories of archeologists, anthropologists, and historians have revealed small measures of this incredible cultural diversity. Evidence from elaborate burial mounds in the Central States to carefully orchestrated burial arrangements in the Southwest points to honorable treatment of the dead. In the Northeast woodlands, great feasts were held to honor the deceased ancestors. In the Northwest, it was believed that the dead had "their realm, or one of their realms, at the bottom of the sea" (Sullivan 1989: 15). Other groups believed the spirits of their dead lived in the sky or in the ground, or even that they may be reincarnated or transmigrated into familiar animals. The consciousness of a supernatural world of spirits and gods led to traditional rituals and elaborate ceremonies performed to honor the departed dead believed to exist in a parallel world. Many forms and interpretations of these ritual ceremonies continue throughout the Native American tribes of today.

Parallel to this ancient world, Europeans began to build their permanent settlements with St. Augustine, Florida (1564), and then a little more than a half century later in Jamestown, Virginia (1607), and Plymouth, Massachusetts (1620). By the close of the seventeenth century, Boston, New York, and other cities had begun to flourish, and the gentry generally followed the funerary customs of the Old World. Nathaniel Hawthorne gave us the unforgettable account of Hester Prynne, laboring with her needles to provide a subsistence living for herself and her child. "In the array of funerals, too—whether for the apparel of the dead body, or to typify, by manifold emblematic devices of sable cloth and snowy lawn, the sorrow of the survivors, there was a frequent and characteristic demand for such labor" (Hawthorne 1980: 86).

During the seventeenth and eighteenth centuries in America, most cemeteries in the Northeast had cemetery markers that featured either a winged death's head, winged cherubs, or willow trees draped over a pedestaled urn. Variants of these designs emerged over time, and one of the later styles featured a cherub with the addition of "wavy and, later, quite curly hair" (Deetz and Dethlefsen 1989: 203). Times and cultural behaviors were evolving from the Puritan norms, and the cemetery stones reflected these changes by becoming more varied and sometimes far more elaborate. Death from disease and famine was not uncommon during this period, and many early set-tlers were unable to survive what was called the "seasoning," or the adjustment period in this new land. Death was also caused by attacks and war with Native Americans.

June 20, 1675, was the date of a devastating attack of warriors on Swansea, Massachusetts. The warriors, made up of many tribes, were lead by King Philip, the son of Massasoit of the Pokanoket-Wampanoags. The attack ultimately destroyed about 25 percent of the English set-tlements in New England. During ensuing battles, British forces were sent to relieve besieged settlers, but many were killed. One of the monuments, just north of Sudbury, marks the place where twenty-nine soldiers were slaughtered. "When the grave was opened for the reinterment, it was described as being 'about six feet square, in which the bodies were placed in tiers at right angles to each other. Some of the skeletons were large, and all well preserved'" (Malloy and Malloy 2004: 57 [qtd. Alfred Hudson 251]). Again, by the care afforded the dead, we see a society that clearly values its members.

In the Chesapeake region, Patuxent Point, a burial site apparent-ly occupied from around 1658 to the mid to late 1680s, revealed to archeologists and volunteers the earliest colonial cemetery reported in Maryland. The site was excavated in 1989 and 1990, and eighteen human graves were discovered. The remarkable preservation of the re-mains revealed striking insight into the burial customs of seventeenth-century Maryland, as well as social structure, diet, general health, and disease of the deceased. Tests determined that the average age at death was 32.5 years. For both whites and black slaves, who may have come from Africa and the Caribbean, early death could occur from dysentery, typhoid fever, or secondary illnesses to systems weakened by malaria. In death, the white and black bodies were buried apart from one another.

Written records from the seventeenth and eighteenth centuries indicate that most early American funerals were held at home, and in the Chesapeake region, bodies were often interred in the home or plantation cemeteries. The pattern for the care of the dead was, again, similar to patterns practiced in England. The corpse was washed, wrapped, and secured in a shroud of wool or linen. After that, "The body would be laid out in the family's dwelling, usually on a board in the parlor, while preparations for the funeral feast [commonly cakes and cider or a rum punch] were made" (King and Ubelaker n.d.: 11). The coffins were usually wooden, and the corpse would be carried in the coffin to a nearby burial place. The funerary rituals were social events, lasting from three days to a few weeks. The graves at the Patuxent Point cemetery probably represent the occupants of at least two households that occupied the site before it was abandoned by the late 1600s.

This early American period became increasingly culturally diverse as various groups arrived from the Old World. In the late 1700s, a group led by Ann Lee (called Mother Ann) migrated to the colonies from England. They called themselves "Shakers" and were a sect branching off from the English "Quakers." A communal society, they lived unpretentious, simple agrarian lives. Their funeral services were equally simple. "The coffin consisted of plain, unpainted pine boards and was plainly lined. At the funeral service, hymns were sung and personal testimonies to the deceased were made by attending Brethren. Following the service the coffin was carried on a bier to the community's cemetery" (Malloy and Malloy 1992: 257). Shaker cemetery stones are often uniform and include only the name, date of death, and age. These Shaker communities eventually closed, but heritage and conservation groups maintain their austere cemeteries.

The Amish are another conservative religious group that split off into their own sect and migrated to the early United States. They first settled in Lancaster County, Pennsylvania, and now number about one hundred thousand in twenty-two states, where they have further

divided into various sects. The *Ordnung* is an oral tradition that pre-
scribes and dictates the manner in which the Amish conduct their
way of life, though it differs somewhat between the different Amish
groups. They continue strict cultural behaviors for their funerary
practices. Then and now, "At death, a woman is usually buried in her
bridal dress, which is often blue or purple. . . . Funerals are conducted in the home without a eulogy, flower decorations, or other display.
The casket is plain without adornment. A simple tombstone is erected
later" (http://www.chaplaincare.navy.mil/Amish.htm).

African American funerals in early America varied according to
the region and local customs. For the slaves living on plantations,
permission to conduct a funeral ceremony was required, but it was
not always granted. Stories about the suffering of the slaves and de-
privation of basic human rights abound in slave narratives. On the
other hand, some owners provided the slaves with their own cemeteries and freedom to conduct their funeral services as they wished. Funerals were frequently held at night so the daily work would not be
interrupted. "According to witnesses, these night funerals were im-
pressive, solemn, and eerie ceremonies." There were pine-knot
torches, mournful hymns, the voice of the preacher, and "graves
marked with posts and, as in Africa, decorated with the broken be-
longings of the deceased" (Raboteau 1980: 230). In the North,
black slaves were usually regarded as members of the family and included in religious instruction and prayers; however, at church services and in the graveyards, they were "still segregated from whites"
(Raboteau 1980: 110).

The Nineteenth Century: Industry, The Gilded Age, and Immigration

Until the Civil War and well after in the United States, care of the
deceased followed the pattern of customs in Europe. Tending to the
deceased was an act of duty and devotion performed by the family.
The body was carefully cleansed, groomed, dressed, and laid out in
the home for a period of time. In some homes in the Provo, Utah, region, there are parlors with bay windows designed to be wide enough

to accommodate a coffin beneath the curtained source of light. Though techniques for embalming were refined during the Civil War (after first being experimented with in France), until then, most bodies were not embalmed, and burial took place within a few days. Friends and neighbors provided foods to sustain the bereaved family for several days, and after a religious service held at the home, a livery would provide a wagon in which to carry the deceased to its burial place. It was not unusual for families to have designated burial places on their own property if they owned land.

The wake, which will be discussed in more depth in a later chapter, was a preventative measure performed so as not to bury the deceased prematurely. Stories of people having been buried alive were not uncommon. Family members and friends would take turns remaining in the room with the body to watch for any sign of life. In the Jewish tradition, this is sometimes called "watching," though in traditional Jewish death customs, the deceased is to be buried within twenty-four hours. Often close family and friends would gather in the home at this time, and both foods and beverages would be provided so the bereaved would not need to be bothered with mundane tasks.

The traditional Jewish custom is for the bereaved to withdraw from the public for seven days. Called *Shiva*, and fully practiced more customarily in the nineteenth and early twentieth centuries, close family members and friends would call at this time with condolences and sustaining foods. In other American cultural practices, the foods furnished to the family might range from breads and ham to covered dishes and fried chicken. Then as now, different ethnic and regional cultures provided the best they had to offer, and the privacy of the sorrowing family was respected.

After embalming became perfected during the Civil War era, the American response to funerary ritual began to involve the larger community beyond the family. Sons who had lost their lives in the war could be embalmed and shipped home by train. Families could hire a wagon to carry the body to their home where final preparations could be made. The funeral industry slowly evolved, and by the mid-nineteenth century, the early rudiments of the undertaking business in the United States, as we recognize it today, were underway. In the early part of the 1800s, the "hearse and the coffin . . . became viable business ventures in their own right" (Laderman 1996: 45). The middle and upper classes of the northern states enjoyed presenting a dignified public face of supposed European refinement, and this desire was not lost on entrepreneurs. Over time, the undertaker began to assume other responsibilities regarding the care of the deceased. Families who could afford it increasingly turned over the tasks of announcing the death, preparing the corpse for the viewing, removing the casket and corpse to the cemetery, and either burying the casket or placing it in the family crypt, to the undertaker.

Eventually, sanitation concerns and threats of illness from contaminated water provoked townspeople to move their cemeteries to rural areas beyond the edges of the settlements. Early cemeteries in New England and parts of the South were parklike areas where people would go frequently to clean family graves and have family picnics. The first pastoral cemetery was Mount Auburn established in 1831 on the Charles River in Boston, Massachusetts. Laurel Hill in Philadelphia (1836) and Green-Wood in Brooklyn (1838) were subsequently established as parklike resting places. They continue to be well maintained and well used necropolises of honor to the dead.

After the Civil War, "The corpse became a commodity in the new funeral industry and entered a complex network of commercial activity" (Laderman 1996: 45). While not everyone could afford to take advantage of the talents of the undertaker and his assistants, the provision of laying the deceased in a coffin, directing the home funeral, and providing the necessary closure supplied a wanted and needed service for many Americans.

During the latter part of the nineteenth century, and on into the twentieth, great influxes of immigrants flooded the large cities of the United States and usually lived in flats or small apartments. Because their homes were very small, the need arose for funeral parlors where the families could have a wake and then a funeral. Though the funeral homes varied from undertakers who used their own parlors for the service to the mortuaries common in the United States today, the mortuary is still the most used practice for accommodating the needs of families at the time of death of a loved one.

Some mortuaries now provide a dining room for family and guests after the funeral service. Gourmet meals are catered and served, and menu variations accommodate the cultural, religious, or ethnic needs of the family. American funerary history and practice, and the rise of the funeral industry, are fascinating and complex accounts. In a nation as diverse and inconsistent as the United States, the funeral industry has developed capitalistically, that is, to earn money, just like any other business.[9]

In America Today

For centuries, for better and for worse, our American people have shared different kinds of boundaries based on social and political history. Cultural and religious differences, ethnic practices, and unfamiliar languages have been demarcated as borders between the various groups. Death, actually the great leveler experienced by all, gives evidence of these boundaries as the deceased have been separated in cemeteries according to these same categories. Many cemeteries have allowed a variety of groups within them, but again, the graves are often segregated into various group designations. This attests to the multifaceted ideological dimensions of American citizens, but it no longer represents the contemporary cultural milieu. We have reached a transitional period of our society; a period that many cultural scholars would call *liminal*. We are at last at a transitional point between two stages of cultural development: Cross-cultural boundaries are becoming diminished, and we have become a people where intermarriage between ethnic groups and/or religious orientation is common. The term "family" is used as a designation for all kinds of interactive groups living together and supporting one another, and segregation is really a travesty of the past. Its legacy, however, holds lessons that must not be forgotten. Along with the growing individualization and maturing of our country and its people, we have moved into an era of adaptation and change.

Most Americans face the world with pride and defense intact. Still, people die. That simple truth touches every human on earth and may seem to some an intuitively obvious reality; yet many contempo-

rary Americans push the concepts of death far from their lived real-
ties and develop a sense of invincibility that collapses in disbelief and
shock when faced with the loss of someone near and dear to them. To
protect a vulnerable, sometimes childlike public from being overcome
with excessive reality concerning death, Service Corporation International (SCI), one of the leaders in the American "death" care industry, has even developed special terminology to avoid the possibility of
depressing, negative, or morbid connotations concerning death. The
following is a partial list of SCI's deathless words:

Casket Coach	not	Hearse
Display Area	not	Casket Room
Interment Service	not	Grave
Opening Interment Space	not	Digging Grave
Closing Interment Space	not	Filling up Grave

(Mitford 1998:194)

A currently popular television series, HBO's *Six Feet Under* is a
situational comedy about a dysfunctional Pasadena family that runs
a funeral home. For some viewers, the show seems to be life affirming
and presents the ongoing negotiations of a large and complex ménage.
For others, the show has diminished the dignity that professional
burial services like to think they can provide for grieving families.
There is no doubt that the funeral industry is a business, and certainly there is dark humor in presentations like *Six Feet Under* (the episodes are now available at video rental stores). However, the crude
language and dialogue—though often funny and emotional and perhaps even educative to an American public largely uninformed about
funerary costs, constraints, and procedures—have a definite Rabelai-
sian essence. For sensitive viewers the episodes may be more disturbing than life affirming as the producers intended. Still, the show has
succeeded in creating a juxtaposition of a lived reality with the inevi-
tability of death that tends to be subsumed unless forced into day-to-
day life.

Six Feet Under has woven various identity ghosts through its ep-isodes.[10] Looking at American identity for a moment, it is significant that our culture as reflected in *Six Feet Under* is frequently pictured in a kitchen. There a mother, caregiver, nurturer, and food-provider creates an interesting juxtaposition with food and dialogue about death, again linking past and present, death and life, in ongoing sym-bolism. Food scholar Sidney Mintz states: "The foods eaten have his-tories associated with the pasts of those who eat them. . . . Nor is food ever simply eaten; its consumption is always conditioned by meanings. These meanings are symbolic and communicated symbol-ically; they also have histories" (Mintz 1996: 1). Symbolically, food has many meanings, and those meanings are flexible. One would not prepare brightly decorated cookies and cakes for a mourning family; yet at holiday time, a plain cookie or cake would, for most families, be equally inappropriate.

The American resistance to death isn't hard to understand con-sidering that we live in an age of advanced and available medical care, increased educational and economic opportunity, readily avail-able world news and transportation, and numberless other perks and advantages that come from being alive and American in the twenty-first century. Most middle-income Americans keep medical and den-tal check-up appointments, save a little of their paychecks, plan for their own and their children's education, and look forward to leisure including almost ritualistic foreign trips (meaning they take the same tours, eat the same foods, and take the same pictures as their peers) in their latter years. Familiar behavior begets a certain level of com-fort for most people, and from ritual behaviors such as coffee and oranges with the newspaper on Sunday morning, to the setting off of fireworks on the Fourth of July, Americans embrace festivity, celebra-tion, and traditional folk behaviors—including of course, construc-tions and behaviors toward death—as much as any other world society.

Death has always brought with it a sense of loss and a reason to create or construct practices and behaviors to provide some level of comfort for the survivors and some sense of security for those being placed in the grave. Archeologists and anthropologists (and folklor-

ists) have looked long for meanings in ancient burial sites and have
repeatedly found the evidence representing caring ritualistic behaviors associated with the loss of valued members of a tribe or clan. As
noted earlier, ancient graves have been found around which stones
and sometimes bone have been carefully arranged; tools have been
carefully placed within the graves; and hunting weapons, finely
wrought jewelry, and food baskets within the grave sites denote evidence of decent and respectful treatment for the dead. Most of the
ancient belief systems have been lost, but importantly, these objects
seem to indicate that there was a primal belief in the ongoing life of
the individual in some form—a form in which artifacts of life would
be needed, including food.

As for our own day, we no longer imbibe the ground powder of
mummies to improve our health as was once done in the medieval
world (and mentioned in Shakespeare's *Othello*), nor do we encase
bodies in jointed jade chips as some wealthy Chinese did before the
Common Era. Still, we do have a variety of interesting and meaningful rituals practiced in the United States in association with the burial or cremation of our dead. Our nation is, as folklorist Simon
Bronner wrote, "a political idea supporting a pluralism of communities rather than a cultural unity" (Bronner 1998: 3). We have great
diversity as well as commonalities, and recognizing and respecting
those likes and dissimilarities assists in establishing a healthy, toler-
ant, national perspective. Folklorists, among other public and academic researchers, collect, classify, analyze, and discuss oral traditions,
material artifacts, customary practices, and belief systems of all human beings. That is, folklorists look for meaning in things people
say, make, do, and believe. Folklore records the unofficial culture of
communities (or folk groups), and it articulates a framework of behaviors for groups in all levels of society from the most humble to the
most affluent. This study is representative of an interdisciplinary
folkloristic approach which opens legitimate avenues of research including materials gathered from traditional research methods, the Internet, folklore archives, and information collected in ethnographic
interviews conducted by the author.

Folklorists have found that behaviors and various artifacts, verbal and material, continue to exist as long as they have meaning to the participants. In the United States, funerary practices differ vastly, ranging from a simple burial within twenty-four hours of death and an immediate return of family and friends to regular daily activities to elaborate ceremonial performances days or even weeks after the death, and sometimes extended periods of mourning. Foods play an integral and unifying part of communal traditions, and certain foods are traditionally used because of the meanings attached to them. From the constant presences of bread and wine at mealtime around the Mediterranean to the ubiquitous use of yogurt and cheese in the far northern countries of the world, to the always-handy ketchup on the table in parts of the American South, foods and food ways weave tight community bonds. Thus, when faced with a shared loss due to a death in the community, familiar foods serve as a soothing balm of community identity, solidarity, and communal connectedness.

When someone dies it can trigger a series of changes for the immediate family as well as the community. In some belief systems, it may even mean a significant alteration of status for a widow, widower, or other members of the household. Along with those changes come adjustments in relationships and responsibilities. To assist the bereaved to emerge intact from the emotional and disconcerting period of mourning and loss, caring human beings, both professional and lay, reach out with whatever appropriate means they can. To assist the suffering from the bleak period of sadness to a period of light and joy, once again, is a process best undertaken systematically and traditionally. There is no need for surprises, but rather it is a time for the calm, predictable unfolding of the familiar, a soul-reviving celebration for the living, performed in honor of the dead.

CHAPTER ONE

Funerals as Festivals

The Irony of Festivity around Death and Its Americanness

There is a striking juxtaposition of mingled emotions in funerary behavior. Grief in sorrow for the absent loved one, and the joy that results from festive reunion and celebratory activities with close family and friends coalesce in the ritual responses to death. The events surrounding mourning, memorial or funeral rites, and burial or cremation require sober reflection and response, but for most contemporary Americans, that restrained period of introspection and sorrow doesn't sustain itself for long. Our culture, overall, does not keep extended periods of mourning in practice. There is ongoing memorialization and commemoration in many of our varied cultural, religious, and ethnic traditions, but even that is often tinged with pleasure for the participants. America is a country that celebrates life. And as a festival is a validation and affirmation of the culture and art of a people, the funerary event is a validation and affirmation of the cultural values and intermingling of a clan of family and friends.

Angus Gillespie stated that a festival provides the planners, participants, and the audience with "renewed confidence, enthusiasm, and pride which they take back to their home communities" (Brunvand 1996: 251). This sense of pride and enthusiasm for loved ones can be taken home after a funeral as well. The funeral is a planned event that becomes a reunion of family and friends, and the experience is carried home in the memory of all of the participants. In Victor Turner's discussion of communitas, we are reminded of the necessity of process in social life. He suggested that "spontaneous communitas," that is, groups that bond together in the "interstices of the social structure[,] . . . flourish best in spontaneously liminal situations— places betwixt and between states where social-structural role-playing is dominant, and especially between status equals" (Turner 1969: 138). Because of our cross-cultural associations, and our interest in supporting one another in times of stress, I would suggest that society establishes intimate group communities, or communitas, as Turner called shared emotional states, through beneficent gestures in times of sorrow.

Our society values vitality and animation, and in a way, the cultural variance of our plurality is like an inviting bookcase with myriad volumes describing the contexts and histories of our many groups. There are descriptions of rites of passage and celebrations in relation to birth and adolescence, to weddings, to graduations, to anniversaries and funerary rituals that invite and welcome our participation and observation. They are categorized and accessible. The vernacular, material, and customary practices are itemized and described, and when reading about our cultures, one can almost hear and feel the various rhythms and tempos. Often, however, there is very little written in the literature about the deep meaning of foods as a part of the ritual bonding at rites of passage.

Cecelia Jougelard, a Basque-American woman, taught that tasting a culture, that is, eating and savoring its food, is the way to understand the reality of others. When I took a group of folklore students, mostly Catholic, to a synagogue to share in a celebration of the Feast of Haman, associated with the Old Testament story of Queen Esther and her triumph on behalf of her people, the women there carefully described the foods that would be served after the celebration and what they symbolized. This deepened understanding of both the celebration of Esther, and of the women who had prepared specific refreshments to be served afterward. The students gained new insights into the homage paid to historical figures in the Jewish tradition, and also they learned that history can be fun. Children were dressed in various costumes at this event, and many people had noisemakers to be used at a certain point in the reading. We need to lead ourselves, our families, and our students (if we have students) to a richer understanding of the festivals and ceremonies in which we are expected to participate, and in which we are privileged to be invited.

Searching many texts in preparation for this discussion, the element I found missing was an earnest representation of our dynamic contemporary response in the United States to the funerary process and the meaning of the celebratory, rather than somber, post-funeral banquets. Beyond traditionally embedded beliefs, I have asked about what contemporary practices surrounding death really mean now. Do they still carry many of the convictions and definitions from the past, or have the beliefs lost the deeper, structuring import in this faster paced, transient world? In the scholarly accounts, I was often unable to find the *folklore*, the sensitive and informal *lived* experience, as literally believed and practiced today.

Searching for folkloristic responses to the funerary process led me back to Mikhail Bakhtin and his discussion of the funeral banquet "as a triumphal celebration and renewal [that] often fulfills the function of completion" (Bakhtin 1984: 283). He reminds us that "characteristically enough, death is never such a completion in the folktale. Even if it appears at the end of the story, it is followed by the funeral banquet (as in the *Iliad*) which forms the true epilogue. This form is related to the ambivalence of all folk images. The end must contain the potentialities of the new beginning, just as death leads to a new birth" (Bakhtin 1984: 283).

The concept of *funeral* is gloomy with connotations of weeping, isolation, and the finality of separation, and yet I discovered by interviewing people and by attending funerals of friends and family, that just beneath that sober surface of respect lurks the American spirit of gaiety and optimism. Bakhtin, in his study of *Rabelais and His World*, an account of popular humor and folk culture in the Middle Ages and the Renaissance, also reminds us that "the banquet is even more important as the occasion for wise discourse, for gay truth. There is an ancient tie between the feast and the spoken word" (Bakhtin 1984: 283). We know that no matter what our personal ethnic heritage and cultural practice, family dinners (no matter the occasion) are shaping events. Participants of all ages listen to one another and learn both wisdom and folly, both sober and frivolous truths. It is through these very interchanges that the culture is transmitted from one generation to the next, from one branch of the family to another; through the process, newcomers—friends and the recently married in, who have been in the family for a lesser time—are informed and enculturated into the circle.

This celebratory nature of the funerary rituals is certainly not unique to America. Buddhist burial practices pay homage to the lives of the elderly. Lenora Chu, an Asian Studies researcher, stated: "In Chinese tradition, services honoring individuals who die after the age of 80 should be considered more a celebration of a rich, long life rather than a time of mourning" (Chu 2000: 1). Americans too, of every culture, lean toward the belief that death is not necessarily the end, but rather, it is a time of change. Death has touched many younger members of our society through AIDS, increased traffic mishaps, and more recently, military action. For instance, concerning teens aged fifteen to nineteen and motor vehicle death, "Rates were steady between 25 and 26 per 100,000 from 1999 to 2001, but increased slightly in 2002 to 28 per 100,000" (http://www.childtrendsdatabank. org/pdf/77_PDF.pdf). Death has returned as a more familiar member of our society as it once was in long past days of widespread cholera, influenza, and other deadly epidemics.

Certainly September 11, 2001, increased American awareness of the potentiality of sudden death. Personalization and privatization of funerary practice has increased. In researching and recording what people do currently, and why, to honor the dead, I found, across cultures, a repeated emphasis on the rituals of the living. These were nearly always gatherings of reunion and celebration after the deceased had been "put to rest." Funerary ritual is a living part of American culture. Jessica Mitford's work, *The American Way of Death* (1963) and *The American Way of Death, Revisited* (1998), opened discussion of funerary mysteries most people encounter when they are too emotionally disoriented to be anything but accommodating. My interviews reflect changing attitudes toward traditional

American funerary practices, and many of my informants stated that they felt that individualized funerary rituals were extremely important in expressing genuine honor for the deceased.

As the American public becomes more informed, they become more deliberate in their choices and decisions. Emotion certainly colors some of their decisions, but as society has become more educated—in part because of the media and in part because the United States has more college-educated individuals than ever before—people have begun asking critical questions about what previously were sacred, unwavering traditions.

A Chinese Funeral Procession

In some parts of our culture, old, established, core celebratory traditions continue with very few changes or adaptations. Even so, with the ubiquitous presence of tourists throughout the United States, various accommodations have been made to satisfy the curious and to draw consumers to an area. American Chinatowns are an example of this accommodation within ancient tradition. In the 1800s the Chinese were sequestered in small areas of many large cities in the United States, including New York, Chicago, Seattle, and San Francisco. In the exclusionary climate of American jingoism and nativism, their allotted space was often less than thirty city blocks with few thoroughfares. Because of the need for more passageways throughout their isolated habitats, they ingeniously constructed alleyways to provide more places for shops and dwellings. The buildings constructed were narrow, but they were often several stories high and filled with multiple rooms. My daughter, granddaughter, and I were in San Francisco last spring for an editor's conference, and while we were in one of those narrow alleyways, we were fortunate enough to have glimpsed a Chinese funeral procession, a part of Chinese cultural tradition. After lunch at a restaurant a few blocks off of Stockton, we explored the many colorful and crowded shops on one of the main shopping thoroughfares. We were tourists, and we knew that the wares were there for our perusal and purchase, but it was new to us and fun. From spin-off designer purses to ivory-inlaid chopsticks and home decorations, we were immersed in a world of sights, sounds, and tastes unfamiliar to us.

From a tourist pamphlet placed in our hotel room, my daughter had learned about a tiny bakery nearby where we could buy fresh, handmade fortune cookies. We walked uphill for blocks and finally turned a corner to find the little bakery located just inside an alleyway. Looking beyond the shop and as far down the alley as we could see, there were tall buildings constructed close together, one after another, and the alley itself couldn't have been more than fifteen feet wide. It was easy to find first because of the deliciously sweet aroma, and secondly because there was a large group of young teenagers laughing just outside the bakery. They were wearing matching T-shirts that identified them as a touring Future Farmers of America (FFA) group from Iowa. They ranged in age from maybe twelve to fifteen, and the laughter was about one member of the group who had unknowingly eaten a whole fortune cookie—paper and all. At that moment she too was laughing and carefully opening her next cookie.

We went inside and encountered a tiny bakery with two women working the cookie presses and a young man selling the confections to a line of customers. The women turned out chocolate and vanilla cookie wafers, which they quickly folded, enclosing the usual paper messages inside. We made our choices from bags of cookies neatly wrapped, stacked, and ready to go. While I was paying for the cookies, we heard the slow, rhythmic, and unmistakable sound of drums floating into the shop from outdoors. The man said, "Oh, a funeral parade; maybe you can catch it." After we finished the purchase and went outside, the three of us could hear other instruments as well. The sound was coming from a little distance, but we could tell the direction. We climbed higher up the hill and were able to see a little part of a festive Chinese funeral procession. We were told later that it usually covers about a twelve-block route following Stockton to Clay Street and then Grant.

What we could hear were crashing cymbals and loud drums, and what we could see from a distance were people walking down the middle of the narrow street in Chinese-style silk robes and pants with unusual coverings on their heads. There were also several walkers in the procession wearing Western-style suits and dresses. Behind them were a few teenagers and others, tourists perhaps, just following along. There were some observers along the side of the street, but not many that we could see. Apparently it was a common enough event that most people didn't pay much attention to it. The brass band at the front of the parade, called "The Green Street Mortuary Band," had turned a corner before we reached the street, and we were unable to see the band at all. It was a beautiful spring day, and I knew from something I had read earlier that the funeral parade is usually led by a convertible with a big picture of the deceased displayed. We missed that, but I am sure it was there.

Traditionally the band, comprised of people from all walks of life in elaborate band uniforms, follows the displayed photograph, and the mourners follow behind the band. The family rides in slowly driven limousines, and the other mourners walk behind and toss "spirit money" to the onlookers. As my daughter, granddaughter, and I watched, there were a few people near the end of the parade tossing the paper money to the watching crowd, but we were not there in time to catch any. I was told that the paper money symbolizes a "toll" to be used for entrance into heaven.

The band, I learned later, with roots tracing back to the very early 1900s, can be hired for around eight hundred dollars to give loved ones a respectful and proper funeral cartage through the streets of Chinatown. These ritual processions wind through the many narrow streets and alleyways of old Chinatown in the belief that they elude the presence of evil spirits with the crashing cymbals, loud drums, and crooked pathways. There is an old Chinese superstition that suggests that if a sharp right or left turn is made, an evil spirit cannot follow because it is only able to go straight. The parade informs the community of the identity of the deceased, and it is believed to serve as a protective ceremony. The traditional belief is that a displaced spirit or ghost is a hazard, and the sound of the band keeps the spirit nearby until it can be properly led to the burial place. The core elements of the procession have changed little, but another traditional American procession, the New Orleans Jazz Funeral, is undergoing change in both sound and security.

The New Orleans Jazz Funeral

When Jessica Mitford, a vocal and widely published critic of the American funeral industry, died, her friends became her funeral directors. Well informed about various funeral traditions and rituals throughout the country, "they conducted her last rites with a combination of sardonic wit and consumer savvy that would have made Mitford proud" (Prothero 2001: 211).

> Pacific Interment Service, Inc., performed a "simple, no-embalming, no frills" cremation in a $15.45 cremation container. But in a wry wink at the suits at the NFDA [National Funeral Director's Association], Mitford's memorial service employed an antique hearse pulled by six black horses to convey her remains through the eminently public space of San Francisco's Embarcadero district, all to the festive strains of a twelve-piece brass band. (*Funeral Monitor* 1996: 1–3 qtd. in Prothero 2001: 211)

As discussed, processions and marching bands in the funerary customs of the United States are not unusual, but among the most famous and lively are those of New Orleans. On a tour of the French Quarter a few years ago, the guide told our group that youngsters playing "anything but jazz" were influencing the traditional, celebratory funeral parades in New Orleans. Apparently the musical teenagers sometimes join the procession and add their improvisations. The traditional New Orleans Jazz Funeral is one of the most unique sights in the South, and tourists continue to seek it out. Black musicians in white gloves and uniforms, brass instruments, and a crowd of followers have become a familiar sight that both tourists and natives enjoy. Over a century ago, both white and black funerals were usually accompanied by music as the casketed body was carried from the church to the burial place. As early as 1885, it was noted in the magazine *Harper's Weekly* that there were "old primitive funeral fashions in New Orleans where almost everybody is buried with a brass band" (Jones WYES/TV). Times changed, and the whites, possibly bored with the style, dropped the tradition. With the rise of ragtime, renamed "jazz" when it moved further north up the Mississippi, the black traditionalists in New Orleans maintained a musical funeral style. As tradition had it, the music played on the way to the cemetery was usually staid and somber, but the music played after the interment (called the cutting loose of the body), was improvisational and lively. Change is inevitable, and there are adaptations and evolutions in the New Orleans Jazz Funeral occurring even as these words are being put on the page. Over time, the processions have become tourist attractions. Sightseers with little understanding of the event have joined the procession as well as youthful musicians who play contemporary music unrelated to the traditions.

The roots of the Jazz Funeral wind back to the secret societies of the Dahomean and the Yoruba cultures of Western Africa. Members of these societies paid fees to ensure themselves a proper burial. There are still societies, insurance companies of a sort, in South Africa where a funeral and burial will be provided according to the money paid to the group. Contemporary practice there ranges from a pick-up truck for a hearse to a Rolls Royce; the more money put into the account, the more elaborate the funeral will be. The roots of this practice date back for generations in Africa. When black men were brought to America either directly or via the West Indies, one of the things many retained from their past was this belief in secret societies and their benefits. As time passed, some of the basic ideas were applied to lodges and other fraternal organizations, and the burial insurance idea was retained. Within much of the core and on part of the periphery of Bourbon Street, the practice of having music during funeral proceedings was added to the basic African pattern. The tradition of music at funerals had some of its roots in the French martial music played in funeral processions. Over time, the procession to the cemetery metamorphosed into the jazz funeral parade. "Throughout the early history of the Crescent City, both Creoles and Blacks had ample opportunity to see such funeral parades" (Buerkle and Barker 1973: 188).

New Orleans has had a reputation for fine food, beautiful people, lively music, and festive nightlife for centuries. It is no wonder that people are drawn to the spectacle of the traditional jazz funeral parade. It meets the definitions for festival and celebration as it gathers followers who form a temporary community. The music proceeds from its first slow, mournful, and soul-moving tones to the joyful sounds of the second line. The waving handkerchiefs, uniforms, um-brellas, brilliant colors, and increased musical liveliness, following the tradition of long established order, raise the experience of the participants to an emotionally tangible sensation. The encounter pro-vides living proof of joyous human triumph over the possible morbid-ity of death and loss. The deceased is put away, and energetic life continues for the living.

In the film *Jazz Funeral: From the Inside*, written for WYES/TV by David M. Jones, narrator Milton Batiste explains that benevolent societies in the late 1800s and at the turn of the century assured the people that they would have a proper funeral and burial provided they paid what money they could. Many benevolent societies were formed in New Orleans including the Odd Fellows, the Society of the First African Baptist Church, and the Society of Sons and Daughters of Mount Pleasant Baptist Church. The societies had bands used both for dancing and marching. As the century turned, the tradition of the funeral with music continued and became reflective of cultural pride and community spirit. As ragtime became more popular, the bands loosened their styles, and the Jazz Funeral, similar to what we know today, was born. Jones suggests that the presence of the bands in the streets of New Orleans also created a black visibility. They wore uni-forms, performed the music according to the established traditions, and in doing so made a clear statement of their presence. After ob-serving the celebrations of the Jazz Funeral, renowned New Orleans jazzman Sidney Bechet stated, "music here is as much a part of death as it is of life" (Buerkle and Barker 1973: 187).

David Jones wrote that the Jazz Funerals survived through the 1930s and the 1940s, but seriously waned in the late 1940s and early 1950s in part because of Roman Catholic Church disapproval. In the mid-1950s, Jones tells us in his film, there was a self-conscious reviv-al, but even so, circumstances regarding the bands were changing. Older musicians had either passed away or were becoming aged, and music styles were evolving into new and different sounds. In 1955, Harold Dejans created the ongoing Dejan's Olympia Brass Band. It has survived and performs even today in part because local musicians of varying experience, skill, and mastery who wish to participate in the brass band audition and then are often invited to join the group. The musicians' performance with the band evolves into more skilled sounds as they practice and participate; therefore, the sound of the band blends and improves. In contrast to the tour guide's comment, Jones also notes in the film that young people in New Orleans are showing more interest in mastering jazz music than ever before. Spontaneous bands take to the streets, and the sound of jazz, performed by impromptu marching bands, is alive and well in New Orleans. Though as Ellis L. Marsalis Jr. notes, "it is common to hear bands play popular songs of the day in place of the longtime standards handed down from the older musicians, and the stately march to the grave site is becoming a thing of the past: Often now the livelier music begins at the church door" (Marsalis 1998: 3). Enjoying the music and action, one young man on Jones's film remarked that he wished that no one had to die to have a funeral!

In the mid-twentieth century, famous jazz musicians such as Louis Armstrong, Jelly Roll Morton, Bunk Johnson, and Kid Ory, marched, played, and improvised at the funerals of jazz musicians. Since then, however, as Norine Dresser discusses in her text on multicultural celebrations, "any New Orleans resident qualifies for participation in this colorful burying ceremony" (Dresser 1999: 96).

> Nowadays, second-line dancers may dance from the church into the cemetery. Carrying an umbrella decorated with sequins, feathers, flowers, or fringe, the leader of the second line struts along the funeral route. Those who follow imitate his exaggerated motions until the line becomes a sinuous snake dance, bobbing, zigzagging, and gyrating through the streets. Sometimes a group of dancers circles a single dancer or duos who perform their own routines. The soloists dance free-form with myriad dance styles: cake-walking, stamping, jumping, crossing of feet and legs, but the second liners maintain their special steps: toe, whole foot, knee flex, and twist. (Dresser 1999: 197)

White handkerchiefs, unfurled and snapped overhead in time to the music, or rolled and worn around the neck or head; white aprons; and rolled up trousers signify to onlookers that the second liners are part of the undulating ceremonial line as it moves through the streets.

"No longer exclusively African American the second line is open to anyone to participate and sometimes grows to hundreds of dancers" (Dresser 1999: 97). Traditions evolve and change according to the needs of the time, but the New Orleans funeral parade carries with it ancient cultural meanings born in Africa and adapted to American life. Though there is an ongoing metamorphosis in style and sound, the enthusiasm of the young, black and white, will guarantee the dynamic presence of the New Orleans Jazz Funerals for decades into the future. But, at the same time, there is a necessity of caution.

A somber note to add to this discussion is one that occurred as the "sad joy wound down." Nick Spitzer, a professor of humanities at Tulane, aptly expressed a startling moment in New Orleans early in 2004. An unexpected shooting in the crowd shocked Spitzer, his wife, and one-year-old, while "at the end of the second-line for Tuba Fats' huge jazz funeral" (Spitzer 2004: 1). "It was man-to-man—a turf war over beer sales, I'd learn later. I was amazed with how many terms for street shootings we have in New Orleans" (1). Spitzer closed his discussion by observing, "Tuba Fats did his part to keep the best of tradition and everybody loved him for it. How tragic and ironic that a violent death over street turf had to be the final punctuation on the second-line that honored his life of giving to people in those same streets" (Spitzer 2004: 3).

The American Cortege

In today's American culture, the funerary procession to the cemetery varies with the cultural group, but in some religious, ethnic, or even political groups, it is an important symbol of status. In many cultures, for instance, the death rituals sometimes become very demonstrative. The funeral procession to the cemetery is a symbol that acknowledges and pays homage to the importance of the deceased, and the more cars moving with the cortege, the more honor is perceived to have been demonstrated. In most American cities, no matter the ethnic origin of the deceased and the family, the funeral cortege claims a right-of-way and winds quietly through the streets to the cemetery.

Abraham Lincoln's assassination in April of 1865 threw the country into a state of extreme mourning. His body was moved to Springfield, Illinois, for burial, and that long, slow trip was immortalized by Whitman's poem "When Lilacs Last in the Dooryard Bloom'd." That was a time long before the television and computer screens had so thoroughly encompassed our American culture. That was the less complicated but violent age of the Civil War, and the reality of death reached almost every family in the country. There were few illusions about the difficulty of survival and the reality of death.

In Mikhail Bakhtin's text, *Rabelais and His World,* we are informed that in the early days of the Roman state, "the ceremon[y] of the triumphal procession included on almost equal terms the glorifying and the deriding of the victor. The funeral ritual was also composed of lamenting (glorifying) and deriding the deceased" (Bakhtin 1984: 6). The tradition of both glorifying and deriding the deceased has continued. In recent history, President Ronald Reagan's funeral celebrations were also met both with celebration and derision. By way of newspaper articles, letters to the editor, and postings on the Internet, many people expressed strongly negative opinions about the event's cost to American taxpayers. The public complained about uncritical tributes that pervaded the American media, given the controversial nature of Reagan's presidency. As the variance in grave markers and monuments within any cemetery demonstrates, Americans are not equal in fame and fortune in life or in death, but deceased American presidents, no matter the historical record, are honored with all the pomp and circumstance that office commands with no expenses spared.

Our society has changed so extensively that scholar Robert Cantwell wrote: "purely imaginary experiences in the video, radio, audio, and tactile spheres [are] so extensive as to constitute for many people the represented reality or 'culture' in which they live" (Cantwell 1993: 278). When President Reagan died, the whole nation was caught up in the acknowledgment and celebration of his death. President Bush called a national day of mourning and ordered flags to be lowered to half-staff for thirty days. Services began with a private family service at the Ronald Reagan Presidential Library in Simi Valley, California, and then the body was flown to Washington, D.C., to lie in state in the Capitol Rotunda. Later in the same week, the body was taken by motorcade to the National Cathedral for another funeral service, and then it was returned to California for a private funeral and burial at the library.

From jellybeans (the former president's favorite candy), to signs ("God Bless the Gipper"), to a myriad of spoken and written tributes, the nation took part through the media in the solemn yet almost carnivalesque ceremonies. Many citizens became emotionally engaged with the unfolding events, and some of that emotion was expressed on their computers. One site on the Internet, "Ronald Reagan Facts," listed information that ranged from his favorite Bible verse and hymn, to his most and least favorite foods.[1] Because photographers and cameras captured many sensitive moments of the funerary process, there were those who suggested that some of the personal scenes were simply invasive, making it as Roland Barthes might suggest, "a spectacle of excess" (Barthes 1990: 15). Cannon salutes, the pomp and circumstance, and the shared sense of loss with Nancy Reagan was overkill to some, and a poignant historic event to others, but our people generously saluted a fallen leader in the manner to which he had become accustomed. Many Americans, as Cantwell suggested, felt that they had become front-row observers, and for a few weeks, the Reagan funerary festivities were a part of their lived, cultural reality.

Funerals are a festive part of the many cultural performances that are ongoing folkways in our American society. The funerary rituals, interpreted many ways, provide a time to abstain from routine activities—a time to gain emotional sustenance through the enveloping of belief systems, close family, and friends. It is, to adopt a phrase from Falassi's 1987 title, which is well known to American folklorists, a "time out of time." The mourners need the closure, and the deceased needs to know, before entering the realm of the unknown, that he or she will be mourned, that the transmutation about to take place will be noted and honored, and that the life lived was valued. As we have seen here, not all deceased are equal, but for most Americans the soothing care given at the closure of their lives is both informing and curiously engaging to onlookers.

CHAPTER TWO

The Final Passage
Rituals for Separating from Life

In a culture as diverse as the United States, the rituals for separating from life are also diverse and distinct. A commonality often referred to lies in the analogy of death and sleep. The living perform the utmost efforts to assist the dying to fall asleep in death as peacefully as possible. The dying very often consciously enter the liminal space between mortality as they have known it, and the ultimate finality of death, with a variety of responses. This still-mortal zone, before the heart beats its last, is a time of acceptance for some and deep resistance for others. It is a time when both the living and the dying recognize a transformation, and it has been described by many as a moment when peace and contentment seem to permeate.

Arnold van Gennep analyzed the ceremonies of mortality or "life crises," calling them *rites de passage*. "He pointed out that, when the ceremonies were examined in terms of their order and content, it was possible to distinguish three major phases: separation (*séparation*), transition (*marge*) and incorporation (*agrégation*)" (van Gennep 1960: vii). Van Gennep wrote:

> On first considering funeral ceremonies, one expects rites of separation to be their most prominent component, in contrast to rites of transition and rites of incorporation, which should be only slightly elaborated. A study of the data, however, reveals that the rites of separation are few in number and very simple, while the transition rites have a duration and complexity sometimes so great that they must be

granted a sort of autonomy. Furthermore, those funeral rites which incorporate the deceased into the world of the dead are most extensively elaborated and assigned the greatest importance. (van Gennep 1960: 146)

I would suggest that the three categories of rites have metamorphosed into a different schema in our individualistic American culture. Our vanity-driven culture has turned many inward, making them resistant to generalized traditions. Though we respond to the incorporation of our deceased into the world of the dead, it is with temporarily engrossed but passing interest. The emphasis that emerges is on ongoing life. The American emphasis on individuality, personal need, and connectedness has taken precedence over engagement with separation, transition, and incorporation. I suggest replacing, or at least augmenting, van Gennep's three stages with *awakening, transmutation,* and *connectedness.*

At the time of death and burial, though there is a solemn period observed, the solemnity gives way to a celebration of nostalgia, memory, and ongoing life. If we look at this process from the perspective of behaviors of the living rather than focusing on the separation of the deceased, it becomes apparent that our celebratory emphasis is on the matter we see, that is, ongoing life and our response to it.

To become human is to be quickened and animated in response to our own real needs and the needs of others coexisting in this contemporary world. Awakening to dynamic human need is a process, and it takes place at different times for different people. Heracleitus, an ancient Greek philosopher who believed everything was in a state of flux, stated that we cannot step in the same river twice. That means that we grow and hear different elements of wisdom in different ways and different times, and we add them to our own behaviors and needs as they are understood. Both our cultural ideology and our traditional American psychology remind us that we must meet our own needs before we can respond well to the needs of others. To accomplish either of those requirements, both recognition and arousal have to take place. That *awakening* can happen any time after a human being becomes genuinely accountable for his or her actions. *Separation* is in direct opposition to this kind of awakening. We are each one individual and separate in our existence, but the *awakening* triggers us to a human response to both ourselves and to others.

To alter or modify ourselves in relationship to our own individuality and to others requires a recasting of perspective, and in the situation of a pending death—either our own or someone else's whom we value—an understanding of the transposition to another state of being becomes a part of the process of wisdom and understanding. *Transmutation* to another state, whether that is becoming a mature and responsible person, one who can and will make a positive contribution to society, or a *transmutation* to a lesser or unknown state as we must do in death, is a concept unlike van Gennep's *transition*. Transmutation is, again, process. It is a step-by-step, somewhat undefinable, amorphous procedure. There are diverse ways of applying the concept of transmutation to our maturation and perspective: some individuals have epiphanies, and some seem to experience almost suspended immaturity. But it is the process of reflectively modifying one's thinking and behavior to reach a constructive and positive personal worldview, and connecting those elements of wisdom to the greater community.

As we become awakened to the necessity of change and pass through the process of transmutation, we become bound in an expanding web of *connectedness*. Transmutation takes place in each of us as we move through the different passages of life, and connections are made all along the journey of our increased sense of individual responsibility. That process can be examined from a linear or circular perspective, but that mutation or alteration from one self to another, amalgamated with the process of awakening, yields a different outlook, a different perspective, a different point of view. The *connectedness* to others that we discover we need appears with wisdom and understanding as we awaken, change, and mature. That is true of cultures and societies as well as individuals. Van Gennep's *incorporation* does not carry the imperative implication of reciprocity. It is incongruous to use both terms, that is *connectedness* and *incorporation,* to mean the same thing. *Connectedness* is to give and to receive according to perceived needs and designs for a universally improved quality of life.

An example of the three *rite de passage* concepts I have suggested can be demonstrated by the personal and family-related events of my mother-in-law's experiences in the course of her last illness and death. She was cremated a few days after her demise. After a "favorite old hymns only" memorial service in her honor, my husband and his sisters scattered her ashes at the seaside where she had spent many happy days during the last few years of her mortality. There was a slight breeze as the ashes were being scattered, and my husband got a piece of the ash in his eye. His sisters, buoyant and happy that their mother's suffering and long struggle with cancer had come to an end, said, almost simultaneously, "Well, lucky you. You'll have a little piece of Mom with you forever!"

Comforted by the presence of her two daughters during her last several months, my mother-in-law enjoyed listening to them as they sang and played old hymns on the guitar. Capable and generous Hospice nurses met her physical needs, and the daughters met her psychological and emotional needs. They sang, shared memories, wondered about future reunions, made family treats for her as long as she was able to enjoy them, and loved her into death. She was at peace with herself, her family, and her body, though she had fought the cancer long, and certainly did not "go gently into the night." The journal that the daughters recorded shows that her last weeks were reasonably philosophical and happy. She never lost touch with reality, and laughed about a new car she bought about a year before her death. At the time of the purchase, she told us all that it was a sure sign of an optimist to make a purchase like that after being told that death lurked just a few months away. She was a brave eighty-two, and believed that she, like Rachel Carson and other favorite authors of hers, would somehow mutate into another form but never quite cease to exist entirely. What was of most value to her, she repeated many times, was that her legacy of gentleness and tolerance be understood and practiced by her progeny. She encouraged life, gentle laughter, and patience for the unpredictability of life. She only asked us to savor life with conscious dignity. Hers was an *awake* life with many transmutations, and we will remain connected to her memories as long as we exist.

Life, ongoing life, is really what death rituals are about. Mourners who are fortunate enough to be enveloped in familiar traditions by family and caring friends can become revitalized and newly sustained by the process. Mourning traditions revive and animate memories and feelings. They satisfy a human need of validation and inclusiveness; that is, we need to feel that we are an acceptable part of a larger whole. We bid farewell to those who have gone to another dimension, and by sharing memories of the deceased, people reinforce feelings and even beliefs about the deceased after the veil of death is drawn closed. Newly learned information as well as personal memories about the deceased are shared with generous and positive caution. The deceased individuals are forever gone and no longer present to defend themselves should a conflicted narrative be shared. That is the reason, I believe, that almost every culture carries cautions and traditions against speaking ill of the dead. The American Navajo tradition carries a further injunction to never speak the name of the dead at all.

As long as we live we are the sole custodians of our own memories, and we have a responsibility to protect our own as well as those of others as another element of the *awakening, transmutation,* and *connectedness* of the human condition. Ritual behaviors are sacred transformations that usher participants safely across unknown boundaries of apprehension.

There are rituals for the dying in all cultures, and immigrants far from their homeland invent strategies of incorporating their native country's customs to ensure their peace of mind. Steve Zeitlin and Ilana Harlow shared an example of ritual maintenance of Indo-Americans in the United States: "In a South Asia neighborhood in Queens, New York, it is possible to buy sealed copper vessels of water from the Ganges. The water is to be sprinkled on the dead who die away from the sacred place to purify them before cremation" (Zeitlein and Harlow 2001: 15). In India, the Hindu tradition is to have one's ashes strewn in the Ganges in preparation to being carried away by Shiva, the Lord of Death. No matter the name of the god, the place, or the time, for most human beings, loving hands prepare the body for its last journey.

Comfort in the Last Moments

In the Muslim tradition, there are centuries-old rituals performed at the time of death to reassure both the living and the dying of the continued safety and well-being of both. At the moment of death, part of the Islamic conviction is that "the dying person should turn her or his face toward Mecca and say, 'There is no god but Allah,' in preparation for the questioning that is believed to occur in the tomb by the angels of death" (Denny 1987: 103). The living believe that angels of death, Munkar and Nakír, visit the deceased in the tomb soon after death. The belief in the survival of the spirit is strong among many of the Muslim faith, and if the preparations are not performed properly, it is said that the living will be haunted by the consequences, and progress of the deceased will be impaired. Harold Coward explained the specific question-and-answer process of the angelic interrogation: The process begins with a command to sit up in the grave in order to answer the questions. The dirt placed over the deceased body at the time of burial is purposely left loose in order for the deceased to meet this request. If the deceased professes a testimony of faith, affirms the uniqueness of God, and affirms the identity of Muhammed as God's prophet, then the test is passed and he or she will be left in peace until the Resurrection of the Dead and the Day of Judgment. However, if the answers are incorrect or untrue, the deceased person's soul will be lost, and the individual will be chastised and suffer *"adh b al-qabr* (torment in the tomb)" (Coward 1997: 54–55).

Because of the strong and literal belief in the questioning of the deceased by angels, precise guidelines for funeral preparation—more religious ritual than social convention—are provided by Muslim faith. These guide caregivers in their response to the dying through the moments of death, ritual washing (*ghusl*), the funeral, and the burial. "The Qur'an and tradition explain the advent of the angels of death who seize the soul at the death-rattle and thrust it, the intervening sleep unsensed, into the presence of the Judge" (Cragg 1964: 208). Great attention and sensitivity is given to help dying individuals through the last moments of life, so they will not falter and accuse or blame God for their misery, or even worse, declare a disbelief in God.

The "Muslim tradition dictates that a person who shows signs of dying (*muhtadha*) should be positioned on his or her back, feet facing Mecca. The room is perfumed, and anyone who is unclean or menstruating leaves the room" (Kramer 1988: 164). If the dying person asks for food, the requested food is provided. Honey, considered a medicine by some Muslims, is offered for comfort. At death, water is dropped into the throat to moisten the soul and make its departure from the body easier. "The soul issues through the throat (Surah 56:83 and 75.26) and is hailed by the angels beyond the point of no return (6.93)" (Cragg 1964: 209).

After death, the body is not stripped entirely at the time of washing, and the washing is performed according to precise rules. In many regions of the United States where Muslims are populous, mortuaries have provided a room where ritual preparations may take place. The body is released from the hospital or nursing home, or possibly coroner, to the mortuary. The bathing ritual must be performed by trustworthy and honest adult Muslims of the same sex. No embalming is permitted, and the body must be washed in a private place. The private parts of the deceased are to be covered modestly during the process, and no comments about the body are permitted. After the cleansing, the deceased is perfumed, perhaps with camphor or perfume, and then the body is shrouded. Sometimes a scent or perfume is put on parts of the body that touch the ground during prostration; that is, the forehead, nose, hands, knees, and feet. The body is then shrouded with winding sheets made of white cotton sometimes imported from the Middle East. This service is sometimes performed by members of the family. An imam (teacher) leads prayers, and the body is then carried to the place of burial.

Sometimes, if local regulations require it, the body is placed in a plain wooden coffin, but whenever possible, the preparations are made for a hurried burial within twenty-four hours, and some Muslims prefer to be buried without a coffin. One of the traditions states: "Make haste to bury the dead person. If he (or she) has done well, you would be doing him (or her) well to hurry him (or her) to God; and if he (or she) had done otherwise, it would be an evil of which you rid yourselves quickly. Therefore, burial takes place before night descends on the day of death, or, if late, the following day" (Coward 1997: 53).

The funeral, called the *Salatul Janazah,* is best performed outside of the mosque or the prayer room (*Musalla*) in the mosque. Some sources suggest that the service may be held two or three days after a death in a funeral home, but, as stated before, the traditional convention is to bury the body within twenty-four hours after death. This is in part to allow the dead to rest in peace, and so family and friends do not grieve longer than they must. Also, burying sooner means that the dead do not have to be embalmed, which is seen as a disturbance to the body. The service can be performed in an activity room or courtyard of the mosque. The imam leads the prayer and asks for God's forgiveness. "The imam stands in front and faces Mecca, while others stand behind him in rows. No bowing or prostrating occurs during the service" (Dresser 1997: 220).

Lauri Patel, a Muslim who assists her congregation at the time of death, said the burial traditions in the United States depend upon state laws and ordinances. The cemetery in her region where Muslims are buried allows only flat, metal markers that have a name and date on them. In New Orleans, in contrast, because of the water table, bodies must be interred above ground, and there are other prescriptions in other parts of the country. The manner of burial is not as important as the caring that is given to the body and to the traditions surrounding the burial (Patel, telephone conversation, February 9, 2004). There are traditions to be observed by the living regarding the graves. For instance, it is strictly prohibited to step on or over a grave, lean, or sit on it. Further, no candles are allowed to be placed on the grave for it is said that the Prophet Muhammad counseled, "Curse those who light lamps on graves." Again, I maintain, as elaborate as these rituals may be, they are performed as much or more for the peace of mind of the living than for the dead.

Ritual ceremonies and behavioral taboos following burial, and other practices regarding the dead, represent boundaries for the living. At some point, most people awaken to conscious subscription to a belief system. That system can be religious, ethical, or philosophical. And humans construct cultural fetters and perspectives. In that finding and subscription, we are both connected and validated, and again serving life, not death.

African American Dying in the United States

As embalming became a more understood and refined process, it was not uncommon for undertakers to perform the service in the home of the deceased. Early in the twentieth century, the practice became common enough that a badge or ribbon would be placed on the front door of the home as a sign to the neighbors that someone had died and the embalming was taking place in the house (Holloway 2002: 19). Funeral wreaths, which are still used on the doors of both black and white Southerners, both inform those who pass by of a recent death in the family and subtly echo traditions of the past. Though St. Louis, Missouri, is in the Midwest, in many neighborhoods there it is still not uncommon to see black ribbons or wreaths with black silk flowers and ribbons placed on the doors as a signal of a death in the family.

The church has played a historic role in African American culture, helping to bring comfort and closure to the living and the dying when life comes to an end. The African American preacher has been known for centuries as an orator who has called the people to faith and repentance through the scriptures and prayer. The violence suffered by African Americans over time has led to more violence and suicide, and faith in things unseen has been taught with power and consistency in black churches. "Even during the period from 1980 to 1992, when suicide rates declined among young white adults, black young men had dramatically increased rates of suicide. . . . Suicides among African American men of all ages rose by 18% between 1987 and 1994 according to the Centers for Disease Control" (Holloway 2002: 90). In her article "Faith Is the Key and Prayer Unlocks the Door in African American Life" (*Journal of American Folklore* 1997), Beverly Robinson reminds us that prayer serves as an expression of piety and faith in the African American tradition. It "epitomizes oral tradition and can be a powerful expression of resistance . . . it acknowledges the importance of each day; and it evokes vocal resolution" (409). It provides both public and private solace during a time of mourning.

Challenges associated with the death of loved ones for African Americans in the United States have ranged from the lack of accessibility to black mortuaries (though some black mortuaries have existed since the post–Civil War era), to limited space, sometimes contested space, for blacks in public cemeteries. Though some contemporary African American funerals are elaborate and expensive in order to clearly pay respect to the deceased, the majority of the funerals are standard mortuary-style events.

African American church congregations are often much more dynamic and expressive in the music and the preaching of the Word than most white congregations. If you have ever participated in a black church service, you may have observed an enthusiasm and passion for the music and preached message that is seldom seen in white congregations. That is generally true. That same difference, passion versus reserve, is present in the funerals and the funeral demeanor of both groups. In the black funeral, there is likely to be loud weeping, touching of the deceased, and even kissing. Regional, social, and economic difference influence behaviors, but overall, African American funerals are more expressive and grief is more openly expressed. My husband's aunt's recent funeral, and my mother's in March 2005 were very unemotional. Both funerals were well attended and conducted by mortuaries and were similarly reserved.

In varied cultures across the American continent, there are practices at death that seem to echo one another with origins hidden in Europe, Africa, and Asia. Repetitions of the behaviors again seem to be practices that comfort the thoughts of the living rather than benefit the deceased. As mentioned before, in the Muslim, African American, Chinese, and Japanese cultures there are traditions concerning the direction of the deathbed and the positioning of the body in the grave. In traditional Jewish practice, as well as in African American and Chinese custom, when someone has died, mirrors and photographs are covered, turned to the wall, or removed to prevent the departing spirit from being confused or even captured as it escapes the expired body. Some traditional Jews think that seeing one's own reflection might make a person vulnerable to the Angel of Death, who is obviously present nearby, and the Chinese suggest that if one should see the image of a coffin reflected in a mirror, there will soon be a death in the family. A clock stopped at the death hour is a practice occasionally found in Muslim, African American, and Jewish cultures, and that practice is mentioned as well as in some Roman Catholic Italian traditions. Holloway suggested that "the practice of stopping a clock was a way of record keeping, and clocks stopped at the appropriate hour were even placed on the grave sites as memorials and tributes" (Holloway 2002: 2).

A Jewish Way of Death

Steve Siporin, a folklorist and professor at Utah State University, once began a graduate class on Jewish folklife with a comment that led to this traditional Jewish proverb: "Judaism was the first monotheistic religion. . . . Everything else about it is diverse; that is, where there are two Jews, there will be three opinions" (Siporin 1990). For those readers largely unfamiliar with Jewish culture and folkways, Siporin's use of the proverb, "Two Jews, Three Opinions," makes more comprehensible the various and individualized contemporary practices of funerary and mourning practices among American Jewry. Ancient strands of historical legacies have formed traditions and practices woven into the contemporary American rituals of Orthodox, Hasidic, Reform, Conservative, Reconstructionist, and other Jews, but the practices are open to individual interpretation among those who are not strictly Orthodox or Hasidic.

For a Jew, life is to be lived, understood, and enjoyed. From birth to death, Jews note and meaningfully recognize the progression of the life cycle. There are specific rites associated with the circumcision of the males, followed by naming of both girls and boys in the synagogue, and then a ceremony called "the redemption of the first born" (Steinberg 1975: 131). The cycle continues through the beginning of religious education, the Bar or Bat Mitzvah at early adolescence, the betrothal (only rarely observed any longer), the marriage, the dedication of the new home, the affixing of the scripture bearing *Mezuzah* (a small case) to a door frame as a reminder of God's will, and then, the rites that "hallow death and mourning" (Steinberg 1975: 133). The period of time from death to burial is called *Aninum*. Judaism is a way of life believed to be sanctified before God, and ritual is its discipline.

There are two important aspects of principles to be considered when a Jewish person dies: *k'vod hamet*—honoring and respecting the deceased—and *nichum avelim*—consoling the mourners. Rabbi Barry Weinstein, of the Baton Rouge Reform B'nai-Israel congregation in Baton Rouge, Louisiana, informed me that he is often with an individual "at the time of his/her passing" (Weinstein April 22, 2003). Otherwise, the family notifies the rabbi as soon as the death occurs. Rabbi Weinstein explained that the rabbi will offer prayers for the deceased and the surviving family members as he or she gathers the family around the bedside of the deceased. Among other prayers, the *Sh'ma* (Deuteronomy 6:4: "Hear O Israel: The Lord our God *is* the one Lord") will be recited, which is the basic "Confession of Faith" and declaration of the oneness of God. If the eyes of the deceased are not already closed, the rabbi will gently close them. Then the rabbi will notify the funeral home selected by the family and inform staff there about the death of the individual. A request will be made that they prepare to come for the remains. If death has occurred in the hospital, the rabbi will let the hospital know which funeral home is to be notified.

For traditional Jews, an intense seven-day mourning period, called Shiva, immediately follows the death. There are exceptions to the length of the Shiva because of employment and the scattered nature of contemporary families, but traditionally, during Shiva, the immediate family of the deceased loved one renounce all worldly activities and withdraw to their homes. As soon as possible, they attend a simple graveside funeral service where a cantor may sing part of the service. The rabbi leads the family in the mourners' prayer (*Kaddish*), and then the family again retires to their homes. In the Orthodox tradition, and in the Hasidic, many customs are observed during this period, beginning with hand washing by visitors before entering the home. There are three supposed purposes for the hand washing: it symbolizes that the visitor has not shed innocent blood, it washes

away the possibility of any evil demons that may have attached themselves at the cemetery, and it removes any ritual impurities that may
have occurred by coming in contact with a dead body. Another tradition is the lighting of the Shiva candle, which will burn for seven days
in honor and respect to the memory of the deceased. During Shiva,
the family metaphorically sits on low stools. Called "sitting Shiva,"
this signifies that the mourners are demonstrating their desire to be
close to the earth where their loved one is interred. It is a symbolic act
of humility of the living in honor of the transmutation of their dead.

Before the burial in the Orthodox tradition, the practice of Kavod
Hamet is honored. This tradition requires simplicity, practicality, utmost respect, and sanctity concerning the deceased person's body.
The ritual cleansing, called *tahara*, is based on Halakha, "religious
rulings taken from the oral traditions and written commentaries in-
terpreting the Torah" (What 2002: 15). For the Orthodox and Hasidic Jew, and for some others, burial takes place as soon after death
as possible, often within twenty-four hours, as a mark of respect. The
ritual washing is performed by women for women, and men for men.
Called *Chevra Kadisha*, or holy society, these individuals who wash
the bodies of the deceased are specially trained volunteers from the
congregation. They are often nurses or doctors. The Jewish community believes that all people are equal in death, and so both the rich
and the poor are clothed in simple linen shrouds and buried in plain
pine boxes. It is believed that God is unimpressed with material goods
and is "concerned only with merits of the soul" (What 2002: 15).

Many Jews feel that someone should stay with the body at all
times until burial, and often the watcher (*shomer*) reads Psalms (*Te-
hillim*) while performing this service. The deceased is usually buried
in a simple white shroud (*tachrichim*) in a functional, plain wooden
casket. Jewish males are customarily buried wearing a skull cap (*kip-
ah*) and their own prayer shawl (*talit*). Miscarriages, stillborn babies,
suicides, and intermarried Jews may all be buried in a Jewish cemetery. The rabbi is to be consulted concerning any unusual circumstances, and though cremation of Orthodox Jews is strictly forbidden,
it is allowed among Reform Jews. Burial is an ancient tradition in the
Jewish legacy. Even Jacob, in Genesis 47:29, asks his sons to *bury*

him in the family burial place. It is an act of loving kindness without ulterior motive because the dead cannot repay the service. To care for and bury the dead is recognized by the community of Jews as a great *mitzvah*, or commandment of obligation, and its performance is rewarded with unsought respect and validation.

There are many aspects of Jewish thought concerning cremation based on the tragedy of history. Traditional Jewish belief suggests that as the body returns to the earth in the simple wooden casket, its very process of decay is a form of repentance for mortal error. Ancient human sacrifice by fire was forbidden to the Jews, and many Jewish people continue to live with the collective memory of the Nazi Holocaust where two-thirds of European Jewry was martyred by fire. Further, as one of the rabbis I visited with stated: "With cremation there are no cemeteries where descendants—if there are any—can come to remember their names and recite the *Kaddish* in their behalf" (Weinstein 2003).

When a Mormon Dies

Mormons (members of The Church of Jesus Christ of Latter-day Saints [LDS]) who have received their temple instructions (or endowments) consider the temple clothing a sacred part of their experience. In parts of the United States where there are no Latter-day Saint mortuaries or morticians, members of the deceased's ward are called upon to dress the body. Members of the priesthood dress male bodies, and women of the women's organization, the Relief Society, usually an officer, dress female bodies. Sometimes, even in areas where there are many LDS people and LDS funeral directors, tender circumstances call for varied family responses and feelings of responsibility toward preparing the deceased for an open casket visitation. In *The Gift of Death*, Jacques Derrida discusses the "history of secrecy as history of responsibility . . . tied to a culture of death" (Derrida 1995:10). There is some public curiosity about the temple garments and robes of the Mormons. For members of this church, the robes are not really considered *secret*, but they are considered to be *sacred*. The white robes of the priesthood, which both adult women and men wear if they attend the temple, are representative of vows and covenants entered into within the sanctuary of the temple.[1]

Usually a daughter or daughters perform the burial preparation service for their mother, but in the following example, the roles were reversed. Kristi Young, a Brigham Young University folklorist, whose twenty-five-year-old daughter, Laura, died suddenly and unexpectedly, shared the following:

> I was able to put Laura's temple clothing on her body. I had bought a new temple dress for her, and it was good to be able to do that myself. Three of her sisters [there are five] did her hair and put her shoes on. It seemed to comfort those three, but the others didn't feel comfortable taking part in that. Just before the funeral service, when it was time to close the casket, I was able to put the veil [part of the temple clothing] down over her face. To me, this was her body, but this was not Laura. Her spirit had gone to another place. It was calming to me, and doing these things for her seemed to help some of us accept that she had completed her work on earth; she had accomplished the mission she had been sent here to do, and it was something to try to understand through our faith. (Young, personal interview, January 24, 2004)

In these varied American cultural representations, we see both similarities and differences in the rituals for the final passage. With care and sacred respect, the deceased are let go, or "cut loose," the traditional phrase used in New Orleans—that is, given over to their final rest, and the families and friends are allowed quiet space to become accustomed to the change in their lives and the departure of a cherished member of their community. The ritual procedures pay homage to the deceased and provide a familiar order and stabilization for the living. Life continues, and in the next chapter, on a lighter note, the discussion will turn to wakes and some of the frivolities talked about and practiced around death in America.

CHAPTER THREE

Wakes and Other Amusements
Frivolities around Death, Including Humor

At the pinnacle of a sacred ceremony, a christening, baptism, wedding, or funeral, there is, as discussed previously, momentary shared harmony. To laugh aloud at such a moment may be a temptation, but it simply isn't done. In 1907, just past the Victorian age of dictated social propriety, James Sully wrote that at those very occasions "in which an unusual degree of solemnity is forced upon us" (Sully 1907: 9), we may be very tempted to laugh inappropriately. Peter Narváez used Sully's comment along with many others to demonstrate that laughter and humor occur frequently in relation to death. In many ways, Narváez suggests, humor assures us of "the resilience of the human spirit" (Narváez 2003: 6). Humor, in the face of death, reassures our fears, helps us to celebrate life, and assists us in dealing "with the enigma of our precarious mortality" (Sully 1907: 11).

We need humor, and folklorists have constructed many theories about jokes and laughter. Is it, as Freud said, a defense mechanism that "can provide relief for repressed energies (inhibitions, thoughts, feelings)" (Freud 1960 [1905]: 181–236 [qtd. in Narváez 2003: 1]), or, as other theorists such as Carrell (1997), Fine (1997a and 1997b), Norrick (1993), and Morreall (1983) have argued, simply "a socially constructed form of communication . . . that expresses pleasure" (Narváez 2003: 1)? It is these and more. We know that laughter often occurs in response to the unexpected, and it occurs when humans have been forced to be sober for an extended period of time. I suggest

that rather than paradox or irony, the germ that makes humor oper-
able is simply surprise. Certainly humor can be used aggressively, but
simple humor based on the unexpectedness of both human foible and
wit is a welcome part of every culture.

For instance, I was close to my Aunt Ruth, a quiet, well-educated
legal secretary and talented pianist. A group of my brother's friends,
mostly Italian policemen, stopped by the funeral home during the
wake to pay their respects. One remarked that Aunt Ruth (Miss Jen-
ner) never really seemed happy. He observed that he couldn't remember ever seeing her smile. In full view of the open casket, where a
solemn Aunt Ruth reposed peacefully, one of the older relatives remarked: "All she really ever needed was a good bedding." There was
a stunned moment of silence followed by hearty laughter by everyone
present. It was a moment to remember.

The comment made was unexpected in part because of the source,
and in part because of the setting, character, and lifestyle of the subject. Psychologically, it was a friendly but uncomfortable visit for the
policemen, a matter of duty, and the comment restored a sense of festivity and warm camaraderie to the setting. It furnished an informal
feeling to a formal situation; an unofficial tone to the almost official
behavior of paying respects to the deceased aunt of a good friend.
Further, the humor bridged a possible gap between the strongly Roman Catholic tradition of the policemen and the deeply Protestant
ambiance of the deceased and the chosen mortuary that served the
Southern Baptist community in that area.

Though one may not think that a morgue would be a stage for
humor, there are people who are comfortable with a form of gallows
humor, a form of comedic storytelling surrounding death. When new
medical students enter some morgue labs for the first time, they are
likely to be subject to unique initiatory rites. Often when newcomers
join a trade or business, a process of friendly hazing both tests and
welcomes them to the work that is unfamiliar to them. Some years
ago, Frederic W. Hafferty wrote an article called "Cadaver Stories
and the Emotional Socialization of Medical Students." Oral culture,
he suggests, that is, storytelling, helps the students in the "transition
from the lay world to the world of medicine" (Hafferty 1988: 344).

The labs are well-regulated places, and these are not literal stories, but rather narratives invented by seasoned students over time intended to shock and surprise newcomers to this initially strange and unusual environment.

The neophytes in the lab are subjected to a variety of narratives related to cadaver and cadaver parts, and the stories serve as an initiation to new rules concerning feelings and emotions in relation to the deceased. Shocking, or supposedly shocking, information encountered by the new students might range from suggesting a chip and dip party using the cadaver's foil-lined abdomen as a food container, to paying the refreshment person at a sports event with a disembodied hand. Other suggestions might include informing a novice that a newly disassembled body is a relative, and these are only mild examples of what seasoned morgue workers or medical students may have in their narrative repertoire.

Because the laboratories are supervised, with strict legalities that must be followed, the events depicted in the stories could not, in all likelihood, actually occur. Still, the stories play an important part in the oral tradition of medical training and emotional socialization of the students; and stories like these emphasize the importance of humor in the induction or initiation process (Hafferty 1988: 346). From tales of fingers dropped in shopping bags, to cadavers locked in sexual embrace, the narrative stories are designed to provoke a reaction in the unsuspecting student. "By telling and listening to cadaver stories, medical student aspirants and initiates construct an experience which is both a source of horror and an emotional rite of passage" (Hafferty 1988: 353). The juxtaposition of this macabre narrative humor with the serious process of medical training suggests again the central part that humor plays in culture. Humor softens tension and helps to make life and difficult situations endurable.

Watches, Gatherings, and Frivolities

There are many cultural constructions that suggest the purpose of a wake. In past centuries, the custom of sitting with the deceased body for the first twenty-four hours, or more, might have served several purposes. The first, of course, was to assure the family that the deceased was really dead. It was not uncommon for people to awaken from a death-like slumber or coma. It was also believed in some cultures that the presence of another human would comfort the spirit of the deceased. On a more practical note, in some parts of the country, it was imperative to protect a corpse from wild animals.

Further, in earlier times unfortunate incidents of being buried alive occurred, both in Europe and the United States. In Beaufort, South Carolina, at St. Helena's Episcopal Churchyard, the remains of a Doctor Perry reside in a brick vault (constructed during the North American slave era, no date). Terrified of being buried alive, he had his friends bury him with a loaf of bread, jug of water, and a pickax. The vault was large enough to swing the ax, but apparently, it was never used (Colman 1997: 20). Another example of the pervasive fear of being buried alive stands in West Point, Highland Falls, New York. In 1902, Egbert Ludovicus Viele was put to rest in the elaborate pyramid-shaped memorial he had ordered built for his wife and himself. He was buried in a stone coffin inside the memorial, which had been outfitted with a buzzer. The buzzer was set up to go off inside the caretaker's house should there be a need. The signal is no longer connected, and the buzzer, apparently, was never pushed (Colman 1997: 19).

Today's medical and scientific technology guarantees that being buried alive need not be feared. The next event, after being certified deceased, is the gathering of friends and family in honor of both the passing of an individual and the continuity of living relationships. Today, a wake usually means a time in which friends and acquaintances may visit the family and pay their last respects to the deceased. In the 1800s, the deceased was often laid out in the home parlor, and flowers or a wreath, decorated with a black ribbon, would adorn the front door. In the United States, Irish wakes, like other ethnic funerary traditions, have made myriad adaptations and exceptions to the traditional cultural mores. In urban Irish enclaves or parishes, elements of the old traditions are kept, and where it is permitted, there is some trend toward revival of the home funeral.

If permission is granted to have the funeral visitation and viewing at home, the casket is usually open and flowers are banked around it. Sometimes a rosary is draped around the hands of the deceased, and there is occasionally a kneeling rail for individual prayer placed near the casket. Women usually stay in the living room, and the men congregate in the kitchen. Though sherry and whiskey are available, the stories of boisterous drunkenness are usually exaggerated. Most of the talk is friendly, ranging over a number of topics including humorous events concerning the dead person.

The old country Irish wake carries stereotypical characteristics known well beyond the Irish coastline. In this ancient tradition, Irish wake activities may include pranks "that ranged from including the corpse in a game of cards by dealing it a hand, to putting a smoking pipe of tobacco in its mouth or even dancing with the corpse" (O Súilleabháin 1967: 171 [qtd. in Harlow 1997: 152]). Many reasons for the jokes at old-time Irish wakes are connected to belief in a literal resurrection, and "as illustrated by the narratives and beliefs concerning the revival of the dead . . . the jokes are thematically connected to other traditional forms in Ireland and thus tie into a broader Irish cultural context" (Harlow 1997: 151). Irish humor often connects to Roman Catholic beliefs, practices, and interpretations. A literal resurrection is one of the many concepts taught by the Catholic Church, and awakening from a deep sleep or drunken stupor might be likened to an awakening from death in a joke. Seán O Súilleabháin wrote that old superstitions come into play most at human crises; therefore, we should not be surprised "to learn that Death, the supreme, crucial crisis in human affairs, was surrounded by a formidable array of folk custom and belief" (O Súilleabháin 1967: 169).

The keening, or lamenting and sobbing, described in O Súilleabháin's *Irish Wake Amusements* text (O Súilleabháin 1967: 130) seldom takes place in the contemporary Irish wake. Today, the solemn funeral Mass is followed by a large family meal where customary fellowship and reunion assure reinforced connectedness between family members and friends. Certainly the drunken images identified with the Irish wake have been repeated over time until they have become a reified perception. In the United States, those boisterous parties have generally been replaced with a more genteel celebration of the passing.

Funeral Home and Cemetery Stories

The need for stories continues over the span of human experience. Those stories, when repeated in social contexts, become folklore, and the stories that last and are most repeated are stories that fulfill some purpose. Sometimes folklore is shared to entertain, sometimes to teach and shape the listeners, and sometimes to warn. The folkloric stories socialize and mold human beings to conform to behaviors necessary for the continuity of their community. Funeral home and cemetery stories are told for the same reason. There is much that the average American person simply does not know about the whole arena of death and care of the deceased. The funeral home is not a place where most Americans would choose to hang out.

Bill Ellis, folklorist and author of *Raising the Devil: Satanism, New Religions, and the Media,* wrote, "One role of folklore is to redefine reality in a way that restores the narrator's control over chaotic situations" (Ellis 2000: xvii). Though the participants may not be conscious of their own psychological or sociological response to the usually unfamiliar stages of mourning, the purpose of storytelling at this time can be one of putting anxieties about the unfamiliar aside through humor and shared experiences. The following stories are only a few among thousands; they are examples of the effect of humor in uncomfortable situations.

Anonymous funeral directors around the United States contributed to a collection of their experiences compiled by Edward Bergin. The short stories range from unusual removal experiences to odd funeral and burial requests. Some are included here, followed by a few cemetery stories, last wishes, and epitaphs.[1] According to Bergin, one undertaker reported that a woman entered his funeral home to make arrangements for her newly deceased husband. She expressed very negative feelings about him and said that she wanted him buried on top of her mother's grave, which was double-depth. Since she seemed to hate her husband so much, the undertaker asked why she would want him buried with her mother. "Poetic justice," she explained: the husband disliked the mother so much, the wife decided to put them together for eternity (Bergin 1996: 21–22). What happens when someone closely knit to your family or friendship circle dies whom you don't particularly like or think you will miss? You may feel a discomfort level tainted with guilt. A story such as this one about the wife's revenge would certainly assuage some unease about such feelings.

It is not unusual for undertakers to receive requests from families asking permission to set up a bar during the hours of visitation or wakes. This is against the law, however, so the answer must always be "no." An undertaker described how one family took matters into their own hands, turning the men's bathroom into a bar. Three types of liquor, vodka, Scotch, and rye, were hidden behind the toilet. One family member was in charge of keeping the bottles full. Both men and women revealed the ruse by lining up to get into the men's room. Many visitors to that wake got drunk and rowdy and had to be asked to leave. After a few hours away they would come back and start the whole routine again (Bergin 1996: 45–46). Here again appears the human tendency to make festive what could be a long, boring ordeal. The usual order of things at social events is to have a few drinks, exchange pleasantries, news, gossip, and jokes (folklore, of course). To create a little secrecy and intrigue is fun for most people, and to have access to the liquor at such a solemn occasion is a delight to tell even if it isn't commonly practiced!

One of the most interesting stories told by a funeral director was his list of funny things placed in caskets during wakes: golf clubs, decks of cards, and bottles of liquor. The most peculiar item, though, was a can opener placed in the deceased's hands just in case he needed to get out of his metal casket (Bergin 1996: 55). But my favorite tale from Bergin's collection is a funeral director's story about a candle:

> When a daughter came up to me during her father's wake to inform me that the live candle next to his casket had gone out, I immediately congratulated her. I told her that when a candle suddenly goes out by itself during a wake, it signifies that the deceased has just completed his or her trip to heaven.
>
> She was so happy to hear this that she told the other six members of her family about it. Before the wake was over, each of them came over and thanked me for conveying the good news about their loved one's arrival into Heaven.

The funny thing was, that I had made up the whole story because I
didn't feel like looking around for a match to light the candle. (Bergin
1996: 53–54)

One of the most delightful things about a story like this one is that
it validates the authority and appropriateness of a white lie. It offers
comfort to humans who nearly all distort the truth now and then for
their own convenience. There are a host of reasons for lying, and not
wanting to be inconvenienced in any way is certainly one of them.

In the funeral industry, the term "removal" means going to the
hospital, nursing home, or private home to retrieve a body and take
it to a mortuary or funeral home. Again, these stories may fall in the
realm of urban lore, but they do reveal a little about areas of work
that most of us know little or nothing about. One undertaker described a trip to a home to remove the body of a man who had died
in bed. Entering the bedroom, he and his partner saw two daybeds
with covered bodies on each. They picked up the closest one, and as
they were lowering the covered body onto the carrier, the deceased's
son came into the room and exclaimed that they were removing his
mother, not his deceased father. They put the mother back into her
bed and retrieved the father. "Amazingly, she slept through the whole
thing" (Bergin 1996: 19).

Another story described a call to remove a body from a fifth floor
apartment. The undertaker climbed the stairs, talked to the family,
and then went back down the stairs to get his partner and the body
carrier. He had glanced into the living room on his first trip and saw
the deceased on the couch covered by a blanket. He didn't think the
man looked very large, but upon removal of the blanket, the two workers discovered that there were no cushions on the couch! The man
weighed between 350 and 370 pounds. Unable to carry him, they had
to drag him down the steps to get him out (Bergin 1996: 27). The ignoble work of the undertakers is thankfully unknown to most of us.

Cemetery Stories

What comes to mind to most Americans when they think about New
Orleans? It is the quintessential party city of our continent. It is a

melting pot of nationalities with dark, beautiful, but mysterious threads of social, cultural, and religious histories. From Cajun to Creole, Native American to African American, the region symbolizes the deepest South with all of its courtesies, traditions, and wonderful secrets. Not to disappoint its public, Old New Orleans is home to some of the most beguiling cemetery stories in America. This romantic city with the intriguing French Quarter, narrow passageways, and hanging moss, the beautiful old homes on St. James Street, sounds of jazz, and the Mardi Gras, is rich in an amalgamation of lore with dark roots in a variety of nationalities from French to Dutch to African. Two stories in particular provide the essence of haunting narratives that have emerged from this tradition-rich urban center. The ancient Saint Louis Cemetery Number 1 houses the bodies of the Voodoo Queen, Marie Laveau, and her daughter, who was also named Marie. Their twin, two-tiered, white masonry tombs "are virtually covered with chalk and red brick markings" (Klein 1996: 102) made by current believers and followers of their invented theology. This mother and daughter constructed ways to practice voodoo. Artifacts, including coins arranged in patterns, herbs wrapped in flannel, bricks wrapped in foil, beans, bones, and other items have been placed on the marble borders of the tombs. When I visited New Orleans just a few years ago, the Saint Louis Cemetery Number 1 was off-limits to tourists because of the fragile nature of the monuments and instability of the ground.

Marie Laveau, who died June 15, 1881, invented voodoo theology, a system of contemporary practice of voodoo, and left a systematic dogma for those who followed her. It is believed by those faithful to her that she comes alive on St. John's Eve (June 23, Midsummer Eve, or the evening before the feast of Saint John, the Baptizer). Through sanctification of tributes, the living are supposed to obtain communion with Marie and the world beyond death on that night. Klein suggested that "had she been literately inclined she may have been to Voodoo what Saint Paul was to Christianity. Nevertheless, her influence lives on in the religion she helped to create and formalize" (Klein 1996: 102). Whether her spirit really returns or not is irrelevant; the important part is that many people believe that it does. The importance of the lore remains because "these legends ensure the kind of behavior which preserves the culture and its values, along with the proper relationships [of the voodoo belief system] without which . . . [their] culture would be meaningless" (Iwasaka and Toelken 1994: 20).

The tomb of Mrs. Josie Deubler, also known as Josie Arlington, a well-known New Orleans madam and proprietor of the finest bordello in the city, is the source of many mysteries. She died in 1914, never having been accepted by the wealthy society as she had hoped to be. She gained a type of vengeance by choosing to be buried in the city's most expensive and exclusive cemetery, Metairie. She ordered a red marble tomb topped with two pillars shaped like flames. Further, she added a beautiful bronze statue, which appears to be ascending the stairs with its back to the family graves in the vicinity.

After completion of the tomb in 1911, rumors began to fly that the structure seemed to burst into flames now and then. After her death in 1914, oral tradition claimed that the statue not only moved, but took occasional strolls. Many explanations of these phenomena have been posed, but it is said that mysterious lights still appear sometimes, and the statue may move occasionally (Klein 1996: 5). More experiences in relation to the strangeness of the tomb and sightings of the walking statue have been recorded as the curious continue to seek a supernatural experience, think they have one, and then tell or even write about it. Humans have always been appropriately curious about life after death. Thus, there has been a constant quest to prove or disprove the continued existence of the spirit (or soul, essence, or whatever one might name it). Returning again and again to places that seem to manifest some otherworldly presence is common human behavior, and the folkloric legends that emerge from these visits are among the most engaging of shared stories.

Last Wishes and Epitaphs

It is a bit clichéd to say that "laughter is the best medicine," but many Americans have grown up with some awareness of the *Reader's Digest*, and the anecdotes in that monthly handbook of Americana have been circulated through American culture for decades. E-mail has largely replaced that source in today's fast-paced climate, and recently my husband received the following motto at the end of a long list of e-mailed Christmas quips compiled by a friend-of-a-friend: "Life should NOT be a journey to the grave with the intention of arriving safely in an attractive and well-preserved body, but rather to skid in sideways, chocolate in one hand, martini in the other, body thoroughly used up, totally worn out and screaming, "Yahoo, what a ride!" (source unknown). There are many Americans who would agree with that.

A will, of course, is the last official message left by the deceased. Many people do not make wills, but taking the time to have one made certainly simplifies property resolution. The will is read when it is too late to be changed, and it often reveals a great deal about an individual and, ultimately, the heirs. Often the will contains unusual and peculiar requests such as the one left by E.J. Halley of Memphis, Tennessee, who had used his own inheritance from his mother to drink himself into an early grave. When he died in 1910, his financial legacy went to orphanages, favorite baseball players, and a sheriff. He also remembered those who had helped him; for instance, he gave "to the nurse who kindly removed a pink monkey from the foot of my bed, $5000.00," and "to the cook at the hospital who removed snakes from my broth, $5000.00" (Lovric 2000b: 31).

Leaving a part or all of one's fortune to animals is not particularly unusual, in that many people leave money for the care of their animals, as long as it is needed, but leaving specific instructions for an animal habitat is less common. One animal-oriented and somewhat eccentric American legacy was that of Jonathan Jackson of Columbus, Ohio, who died around 1880. Jackson apparently had a great love for cats. He left detailed plans for the construction of an elaborate cat home including a dormitory, a refectory, an infirmary, a conversation area, climbing roofs, rat-holes, and a music auditorium "where inmates were to be assembled daily to listen to an accordion player" (Lovric 2000b: 50).

Epitaphs

Most people hope to be remembered well after death, and perhaps the primary source of anxiety about finality itself is the thought of that hope not being fulfilled. One of the great philosophical theologians of the twentieth century reminded his readers that the ultimate anxiety about death is the dread of being "eternally forgotten" (Tillich 1963: 24). Over the centuries, epitaphs have been read as both blessings and curses to the memory of the deceased. From monuments surviving since ancient Greek and Roman times to Shakespeare's Benedict (*Much Ado about Nothing* V:1, 109), from named murderers of the deceased carved in early New England gravestones (Malloy and Malloy 1999: 211) to contemporary verses written for our fallen American leaders, epitaphs are statements, sometimes coined before death, sometimes designed by one's survivors, of the human desire for some form of remembrance after death.

There are numerous collections of epitaphs available to readers, so I will only include a few humorous ones in these pages. It is fun to come upon them in cemeteries, and recognize, as J. Joseph Edgette wrote, that the words and images convey a lot about the departed person and, "in some cases, serve as insights into their individual personalities" (Edgette 1989: 87). Definitions of precisely what an epitaph is can vary, but it usually comes down to some form of written words on a tombstone or crypt. Sometimes they are funny, like the Julian C. Skaggs marker that Edgette found in West Virginia, which reads: "I made an ash of myself." Others are more serious messages such as "Gone but not forgotten." The words can vary from scriptural verses, simple poems about life and death, and maxims, to short paragraphs that tell a story somehow related to the deceased person buried there.

In the cemetery near the Bowling Green State University campus, there are two side-by-side upright granite gravestones with poems written on their backsides. The monuments are tall enough to make a striking presentation, and they mark the burial place of two teenaged girls killed in an automobile accident on the night of a prom. Eerily, the girls had each written poems about early death a few months before the accident, and the parents of the girls (who were not sisters) had the poems engraved on the backs of the monuments as a tribute. Their dates, two young men, were also killed in the accident. One is buried nearby, and one is buried elsewhere.

For many families, the cost of having lengthy epitaphs engraved on cemetery stones is prohibitive; therefore, epitaphs have become more a legacy from the past than a contemporary practice. There is a cemetery stone in the Provo, Utah, cemetery that states, "I told you I was sick," and another there of a gentleman who had two wives that states, "He Deserved a Rest." The gentleman's wife, who preceded him in death, reads, "You're going to miss me when I'm gone." These reflect an active sense of humor among these devout Mormon settlers. Other epitaphs may reflect more about those who wrote them than the deceased. Examples of these come from another of Michelle Lovric's collections, this one focused on cemetery stone engravings. A stone in Connecticut reads: "Here lies the body of Jonathan Stout. / He fell in the water and never got out, / And still is supposed to be floating about" (Lovric 2000a: 13). Another unusual epitaph in Skaneateles, New York, reads: "Underneath this pile of stones / Lies all that's left of Sally Jones. / Her name was Lord, it was not Jones / But Jones was used to rhyme with stones" (Lovric 2000a: 14).

Epitaphs can reveal a great deal about the character of the deceased and continue to serve as a reminder of a real human life lived and spent. Visitors to the cemetery often pause and reflect as they read and ponder the simple words chosen to represent a life. Symbols, as well, can tell a story. The marker of a Jewish convert to Mormonism reflects the pride of his ancient Judaic heritage and the traditional symbols of his adopted faith. The Star of David and the menorah represent his birth belief system, and the Mormon temple and dates of his family temple ordinances and sealings attest to his serious commitment to his faith found in mortality.

Humor in Mexican and American Celebrations of the Day of the Dead

Death and festivities are not unusual companions in Mexico. Ancient traditions of the indigenous Mexican people continue to carry the belief that the souls of the dead return each year to their living relatives in joyful reunion. Though originating in ancient settlements, celebrations of the believed spiritual visitations continue in many urban and rural locations in contemporary Mexico during the *Dia de los Muertos* (the Day of the Dead). These celebrations are growing more prevalent in the United States as the Mexican American people become a larger part of the population north of the border. Scattered Mexican communities and their celebrations have become strongly influential in American culture, and celebrations of Halloween (October 31), All Saints' Day (November 1), and All Souls' Day (Day of the Dead, November 2) have been combined and observed in North American celebrations from college campuses to church gatherings.

In pre-Hispanic Mexico, the *calaveras* (skull) carried complex meanings, and it remains the ubiquitous symbol of traditions and celebrations related to the Day of the Dead. "The skull—symbol of death—was a promise of the resurrection. Before the conquest, death was obsessively represented in stone, clay, gold and other materials" (Carmichael and Sayer 1992: 9). Two months in the ancient Aztec calendar were devoted to the dead: the ninth month to dead infants, and the tenth, which included a great feast, to dead adults. But it remains unclear "to what extent these pre-Hispanic festivals and their associated rituals were transmuted onto the Christian festivals [of today]" (Carmichael and Sayer 1992: 33). The customs and elements of modern belief are clearly derived from historical practices of the past. For the pre-Hispanic Mexican people, death was regarded as a welcome journey. Not unlike in the teachings of other philosophies (Hindu, Buddhist, Christian), life in the Aztec belief system was perceived as a dream, from which the dreamer could only awaken to eternal reality through death.

All Saints' Day, November 1, was set aside in C.E. 732 by Pope Gregory III to honor saints enjoying life in heaven by performing a memorial Mass in their behalf. The date is somewhat syncretic as it coincided with an ancient Celtic festival day, Samhain, a boundary day between summer and winter. In the 1300s, November 2, All Souls' Day, was added to the Roman Catholic liturgical calendar and established as a time to celebrate all dead people. In predominately Roman Catholic countries many celebrations take place on these days, including the Mexican *Dia de los Muertos*. After the Conquistadors brought Roman Catholicism to the Americas, the Church holy days became a part of the indigenous people's traditional practice. Celebration of the Day of the Dead evolved from a syncretism of the native's respect for the dead and ancient Celtic and Roman Catholic roots.

Traditionally, Mexican families celebrate the Day of the Dead by going to the graveyards, cleaning the graves, decorating them with candles and marigolds (*zempasuchil*, a Mexican Indian flower symbolic of the dead), burning incense, and spending the day in prayer and thoughts of the dead. Picnic baskets are taken, and the traditional custom, less practiced now, is to picnic on and around the burial site. Both charming and disturbing myths, legends, and folktales related to this day are shared, including the legend of "La Llorona" (The Weeper). Once a beautiful Mexican woman and mother, who was betrayed by her Spanish love, murdered their children. Now wearing a flowing white gown, she haunts the living in revenge for the loss of her happiness. Many variants of this story circulate, and some scholars (Janvier 1910: 162–65) trace the story back into Mexican antiquity. Stories of the appearance of ghosts or spiritual figures suggest to listeners the promises of continued life and communication after the grave. Stanley Brandes has argued that the Mexican Day of the Dead is not as much about a historical derivation of the holiday, but rather, its "*attributed* derivation and connection to Mexico" (Brandes 1998: 364). It has become, in addition to the festive behaviors and foods, representative of the attitude toward death that symbolizes Mexico itself (Brandes 1998: 365).

During the last days of October and the first days of November, images of the skull (calaveras) are common throughout Mexican culture, and the skull remains the primary metaphor for humor associated with death. Death is perceived and accepted as an inevitable visitor by many Mexicans who have inherited a historical and philosophical ambivalence about the finality of life. On the other hand, there is much satire and irony among the intellectuals toward this celebration, and to give a friend or relative a skull with their name written on the forehead is common practice. "It is hard to imagine a more graphic representation of combined humor and aggression than that embodied in this type of *calavera*" (Brandes 2003: 223). The printed calaveras, a different representation and poetic form of expressing the grim humor of death, is marked by social satire and mock epitaphs presenting a variety of meanings. A metaphorical and literary skull, the poetry might turn toward praise and admiration, politics, strength or weakness, the power elite, or even anticlerical satire. The Day of the Dead is a time to protest perceived and real oppression through the use of humor.

On the topic of wealth and prestige, this calavera, printed in a Veracruz newspaper in the early days of the Mexican Revolution (1910–1920), both describes and satirizes the feelings of the people:

I Am Not Going
Go to the cemetery? For what?
It would be foolishness for me
to go to see so many widows
in mourning and remorseful,
in front of so many other tombs
where their little fossils rest
adorning them with flowers,
placing down *siemprevivas,*
cockscomb, gardenias,
Orchids and daisies
Purchased God-knows-how
and with what kind of money [*pastilla*],
[only] to look at them afterwards,
laughing wide-mouthed
together with those people, who are
substitutes for the deceased in caresses.
Go to the cemetery? For what?
To see so much hypocrisy?
I am not fond of observing
That false weeping,
I don't want to see the pain
without the daughter's consolation,
which is before the father's tomb
is manifested on this day,
only a little later to see her
on the streets and avenues,

prostituting that name which
watches over that cold tomb.
Go to the cemetery? For what?
To see certain ladies showing off
flashy suits
when in this place they should
attend, if not dressed in mourning
because they won't be seen as beautiful,
at least not showing off
that respect for the deceased and
their families is of little importance?
No, *marchantes,* I am not crazy,
if through my misfortune and the
misfortune of many others
we live in the *invieta,*
the city is a cemetery,
from the vegetable gardens
to near Vergara,
where the stamps [*timbres*] of many names
killed on these days sleep without life.
(*La Opinion,* Veracruz [qtd. by Brandes 2003: 236–37])

The traditional observance of the Day of the Dead, November 2, like celebrations around the world, means different things to different people. For the intellectual elite, it is a time of satire and jocular humor in honor of the tragic history of their country. For many urban dwellers, both in Mexico and the United States, it is largely a time to party with a theme. And for the rural Mexican people, as well as the newer immigrants to America who have come from deeply traditional regions of rural Mexico, it is a day to remember and pray for the journey of the dead—to wish them well with drinks and favorite foods, and to hope that they in return bear good wishes for the living.

Italian Humor and Death

Camille Paglia, an Italian American and a professor of humanities at the University of the Arts in Philadelphia, has given an account of the roots of some traditions that remain consistent in Italian American culture. She writes: "I was raised with respect for, but not fear of,

death. Italians dread incapacity and dependency, not extinction."
Speaking of Italian realism, she argues that the roots of that view
were formed by "the primitive harshness of agricultural life, where
food, water, shelter and sex are crucial to survival." This Italian realism is clearly expressed in *The Godfather* films. Focusing on certain
images from the first two parts of Francis Ford Coppola's *The Godfather*, Paglia asserts that the attentive viewer can see that "Coppola
constantly intercuts images of food and death to suggest the archaic
Italian, or rather pre-Christian, cycle of fertility, destruction and rebirth" (Paglia 1996: 2, 5).

In one scene, Peter Clemenza (Richard Castellano), is reminded
by his wife not to forget to pick up some cannolis. Later that day, moments after a gangland-style execution that took place while he had
his back turned, he remembers the white box of cannolis, by this
point on the front seat next to the bloody corpse, and "primly carries
the pastries away" from the scene. With grisly and ironic humor, another food scene from *The Godfather* reinforces the centrality of food
in the Italian American experience:

> One of *The Godfather*'s most gruesome rub-outs occurs at Louis' Res-
> taurant, "a small family place" in the Bronx where the first unsuspect-
> ing target, a Mafia chieftain, advises the other, a corrupt police
> captain, "Try the veal—it's the best in the city." Moments later, Mi-
> chael Corleone, their dinner companion, shoots them both in the face.
> The astonished captain, laden fork raised over his bib, chokes and
> gurgles as if still chewing, then slams head first on the table, bringing
> everything down with a huge crash. As Michael flees, we can see the
> overturned table stained with red splotches that could be wine, to-
> mato sauce or blood—or perhaps, in the Italian way, all three. Cop-
> pola then inserts a montage of headlines with real police photos of
> blood-drenched gangland executions, ending with a shot of a big
> bowl of leftover spaghetti being spooned into a garbage can. *Sic tran-
> sit gloria mundi.* (Paglia 1996: 7)

Certainly a popular and entertaining juxtaposition of foods and
nauseating violence, Coppola's representation of "death Italian style
is a luscious banquet, a bruising game of chance, or crime and pun-
ishment as pagan survival of the fittest" (Paglia 2003: 8).

A Little Touch of Irish Humor at Death

The next chapter, "Funeral Biscuits and Funeral Feasts," will take a lighter turn toward foods and celebrations of the living in honor of the dead. But, first, there was a humorous story printed in the *Milwaukee Journal Sentinel* about an Irish American named Mike Cortright that has a familiar ring for many Americans. Church suppers are popular within most of the belief systems I investigated in my research. They are often fund-raisers, and members of the congregation work long hours to pull the dinners together. Many church groups have raffles, auctions, or even dance demonstrations to enhance the evening and raise funds for the church or often for their private schools. The dinners range from a "bring anything" menu, to alphabetized assignments, to carefully planned gourmet dinners. The common denominator is that they are nearly always delicious, generous, and the desserts are often tried and true family traditions well worth waiting for. Karen Herzog, of the *Journal Sentinel* staff, wrote a story about funeral meals, and included an enjoyable anecdote about her Uncle Mike:

> My Uncle Mike was buried with a fork in his hand.
> As mourners filed past his casket during the visitation, there were more than a few raised eyebrows and whispers.
> "What's with the fork?" everyone wanted to know.
> The answer was printed on a piece of paper near the casket. It was a young woman's last wishes to her pastor, passed around on the Internet and ultimately embraced by my uncle, Mike Cortright.
> "In all my years of attending church socials and potluck dinners," the woman had told her pastor, "I always remember that when the dishes of the main courses were being cleared, someone would inevitably lean over and say, 'Keep your fork.' It was my favorite part because I knew that something better was coming . . . like velvety chocolate cake or deep-dish apple pie."
> "So, I just want people to see me in that casket with a fork in my hand and I want them to wonder, 'What's with the fork?' Then I want you to tell them: 'Keep your fork . . . the best is yet to come.'"
> Maybe heaven isn't a slice of deep-dish apple pie. But death and food are inextricably linked, regardless of what you believe about the hereafter. Where there is grief, there is food—and usually lots of it. (Herzog 2002: 1, 2)

This story, widely circulated on the Internet, has been picked up and circulated in a variety of ways, entering the cultural discussion as urban lore. A few months ago I attended a Mormon, or Latter-day Saint, church service in a nearby town with a friend. A young woman, new to the congregation, had been asked to give a talk in order that the congregation could become acquainted with her. In the course of her talk she mentioned that she collected interesting narratives as a hobby, and she told a variant of this same story. It resonated with the congregation because it was affirmed with laughter and whispers of agreement.

The collective memory of shared dinners and delicious desserts in the church supper context is, for most, a pleasant one. Not limited to the United States, both ceremonial and participatory group meals are ubiquitous around the world. In some cultural traditions, both in Europe and the United States, the immediate family fasts for a period of time before the burial (and also on the birthday of the deceased and the anniversary of the actual death). The sacrifice of food for a period of time can make a funeral banquet and desserts look even more inviting.

Mike's wish, based on his fond response to another's Internet account, reminds us all of the influence technology is playing in our lived behaviors. We live in a huge world made increasingly interactive and seemingly smaller by the technological miracles of the Internet and e-mail. As the young woman told the story to her congregation, I wondered how many were there who had already been familiar with some variant of the story. And further, how many people would incorporate the fork motif into their own funerary wakes and celebrations?

CHAPTER FOUR

Funeral Biscuits and Funeral Feasts
Foods for Hope and Comfort

Throughout the world, funeral rites and associated foods—even feasts—have been a traditional part of behavior associated with responses to the spiritual and sacred nature of death. With elements common to all cultures, foods affirm identity, strengthen kinship bonds, provide comfortable and familiar emotional support during periods of stress, and gently introduce outsiders to lesser-known culinary worlds. There are emotional and socially significant meanings of food, and common foods of the everyday table translate into cultural expectations and markers at signal meals. A common example of that relationship would be the bread and wine present at the lunch and dinner tables of many southern European Roman Catholics, Greeks, and derivative American cultural groups. These are ancient foodstuffs with deep, spiritual meanings that have assumed the Christian associations of sacrifice and atonement. In many of these southern European cultures, for example, Italian, French, Basque, or Spanish, during the pre-funeral mourning period and then at the funeral dinner following the burial, the presence of bread and wine is expected. For many who have come to America from those parts of the world, the sacrament of Communion is taken at the funeral Mass, and the presence of these symbolic elements as part of the funeral meal is simply assumed. Their absence would present an alien, disconcerting message.

In the first three centuries of the United States, Europeans, Africans, Asians, and American Indians shared culinary ingredients,

ideas, and techniques. In *America Eats: Forms of Edible Folk Art,*
William Weaver states that "the 'classical' folk cookery of early
America was based on connectedness, and affiliation with place, a
direct link with nature, and a strong bond between people. These are
qualities that go beyond time and cultural boundaries" (Weaver
1989: xv). Funeral ritual and folkways, including foods, have often
become culturally synergetic, even commodified, but in spite of ac-
culturation and syncretism, there remain distinct food and ritual traditions practiced by various religious and ethnic groups in the United
States. Many of these have been reinforced by the large influx of immigrants since the 1960s. These distinct traditions traverse regional
boundaries and remain culturally specific in the midst of American
intermingling.

Americans are familiar with regional foods such as clam chow-
ders from New England, hearty chili from Texas, the Mexican American flavors of Arizona and New Mexico, Key lime pie, and foods
that represent the tidewater or coastal South. In the late twentieth
century and on into the twenty-first, themed fast-food restaurants
have appeared in every city and state in the Union, and one can obtain foods ranging from fresh lobster to seasoned game in better restaurants with very little effort. The foods served are not necessarily
authentic representations of regional foods, but because they are generally what the public thinks the foods should look and taste like, the
patrons fill the tables.

On the other hand, religious and ethnic groups treasure and even
guard some of the recipes that have been used for generations in their
cultural milieu. The post-funeral feast, or banquet, present in some
form or another in nearly all of the American traditional groups, is
provided in part to meet the needs of the funeral guests before they
depart for their various destinations. Though varied foods may be
served, there are symbolic meanings to many of the dishes, and like
the bread and wine in the southern European tradition, their presence is simply expected. The traditional foods, further, may ultimately serve a variety of purposes.

For instance, in the Utah County region, south of Salt Lake City
in northern Utah, the tradition of serving a potato-cheese casserole at

post-funeral dinners has become a symbol and folkloric practice in the last decade or so. Nicknamed "funeral potatoes," the dish has become an expectation at the funeral meals in this region. That is not to say that it doesn't appear in other parts of the country. I have seen a recipe book from a women's Methodist Church group in Michigan that has a similar scalloped potato recipe likewise named "cheesy funeral potatoes." The dish is so well known in Utah that the 2002 Olympic souvenirs included a cloisonné charm with funeral potatoes pictured on it. (There was another enameled souvenir charm that featured a likeness of Utah's popular green Jell-O.) Several articles have been written about the potatoes in local newspapers and magazines, and many Utah cooks have a variety of different recipes for this expected, traditional dish. Because they are a filling and mild food, at least one large LDS (The Church of Jesus Christ of Latter-day Saints) family has begun a tradition of including the cheesy potato recipe at all family baptisms. (Children in the LDS faith are usually baptized by immersion when they are eight.) Accordingly, this family has renamed the potatoes "baptism potatoes" (Young, personal interview, January 24, 2003). The dish has become a tradition for the living, and many people just smile when funeral potatoes are mentioned.

That food somehow aids the departed is an ancient belief. From the earliest evidences of human behavior, from pyramids to stone tombs in caves, food has been left at the burial place for the sustenance of the dead in their spiritual state. Perhaps the belief was that these substances somehow became transformed from material to spiritual in order for the dead to partake, and in many cultures (Mexican, Eastern European, Italian), the practice of leaving food offerings at the graveside continues. On the other hand, in some cultures of the world, such as Islamic, the ritual practice of leaving food on or beside the grave was and is strictly forbidden. Most American cemeteries have strict rules about what may and may not be left in the cemetery in tribute to the dead. Engaging and provocative differences in response to death emotionally, spiritually, and materially inform us about beliefs and behaviors people value. It has become a priority in this increasingly interactive and multicultural society to become respectfully informed about one another. More than ever before, many

Americans work, play, grow older, and eventually die trying to understand one another and one another's cultural and ethnic differences.

In Early America

In eighteenth-century colonial America, Euro-Americans lived in
small villages that dotted the rural, eastern countryside, and their traditions reflected Old World funeral practices. This was also true for
the African Americans who brought with them ritual customs born in
their homeland, familiar traditions that they believed must be faith-
fully preserved. Both groups carried rites and ceremonies as links with
the dead—and they instituted them believing that the dead watched
to ensure that the ancient traditions were continued. In ancient New
England forests, tribal Americans practiced prehistoric ancestral traditions of leaving foods and various artifacts near the graves to assure
the dead of continued respect and to keep their spirits from intruding
on the living. Varied use of food was part of the death ritual in all of
these traditions, and food continues in contemporary times to provide
comfort, symbolic communal expression, and ritual links between the
mourning and the deceased.

The Europeans in early America would have been familiar with
a funeral custom practiced both in Great Britain and on the Continent: the simple one of passing out a funeral token, often a molasses
cookie called a "funeral biscuit," to the people attending the funeral.
Though many funeral tokens were used as reminders to the mourners
of the deceased (white mourning gloves, a broadside, a copy of hymns
sung at the graveside, elegiac verses, and religious pamphlets), the
most common token was this small cookie stamped with various
symbolic motifs such as hearts or cherubs. A more focused discussion
of this tradition will be included later in this chapter, and it will explain how the funeral biscuit offers evidence of crosscultural connectedness among Europeans in the early colonies. Yet for whom
were these traditions established? I believe these were customs for the
living. The customs reminded the living of the honored dead.

African Americans in the North and South represented other evidence of transmitted and synergetic mourning rituals. Performed

separately and privately—even secretly for the protection of both the living and the dead—the forbidden sounds of drums beat out ancient rhythms from their homeland in honor of the dead; and African American spirituals from that time such as "I'll Fly Away" reflect sadness and yearning for another life. A common belief threading through the African culture in young America was the hope of turning into birds, even buzzards, at death so the slaves might "fly right back tuh Africa" (Brewer 1968: 309). The belief provided hope. "'Flying away,' signifies a yearning for freedom which has permeated African-based culture over the last four centuries. Also called 'stealing away,' it is the desire to escape to a better place" ("Fly Away" 2, 3). Other African American spirituals, including "Get Away Jordan," "Now Let Me Fly," "You May Bury Me in the East," and "View the Land," reflect this same desire, and need, to escape to freedom.

Foods used by the African American people began to carry deep communal meaning for both the living and the dead. In early Louisiana, for instance, some blacks believed that if they placed rice on the graves, it would keep the dead from catching their hoe and spoiling their rice (Brewer 1968: 298). Today, foods used in the deep South since the earliest days of the country still evoke nostalgia for the strong ties of black communities before the African American diaspora to the North. At traditional African American funerals, there remain many expected and featured foods deeply rooted in southern flavors, such as greens, fried chicken, corn bread, and yams—staple foods that helped the people survive and also bound them together in comfort and familiarity.

Native Americans in early New England, mostly displaced and dwindling in numbers, also had ancient patterns, foods, and mourning rituals related to their dead. There were large populations of Algonquian, Iroquoian, and Siouan-speaking tribes in the Northeast Woodlands, and they all practiced both hunting and horticulture to one degree or another. Game was the staple food for all, but in addition there were prominent foods called the "three sisters"—beans, squash, and maize—which were celebrated and praised in ceremonies throughout the year. Cremation was practiced by Native Americans, and feasts, where game and the "three sisters" were served, were arranged in honor of the dead. There are between five hundred and six hundred registered American tribes in today's United States, and the decent and respectful treatment of the dead is various, but the gathering and feeding of family and friends continues. Though most tribes respond quietly to death, many have traditions of providing food for the gathered family. Corn is usually present as well as fry bread and beans.

In the American West, the Hopi used maize as the dominant symbol of their spiritual life. Discussing this tradition, anthropologist Peter Whiteley wrote: "Two perfect ears of white maize are given to a newborn child as its 'mothers'; when a person dies, ears of blue maize similarly accompany him on his journey beyond life. Maize seeds, ears, tassels, milk, pollen, and meal all serve as sacramental elements in differing contexts" (Whiteley 1989: 56).

The funeral biscuit, the sprinkled rice, and the ears of blue maize served as part of a code representing understood messages. Mary Douglas wrote that "if food is treated as a code, the messages it encodes will be found in the pattern of social relations being expressed" (Douglas 1972: 61). The early American funeral biscuit crossed boundaries of ocean, culture, and time, and created a commonality, a code, so *common* as to be almost unnoted and forgotten. The commonality of that little biscuit was not unlike the use of the American flag; they are both symbolic representations of valuable memories. The biscuit became a symbol to keep and to remind the living that a valued member of their circle had died. The deceased may have been a parent, friend, or a child, but the memory of that life was worth keeping. Symbols such as familiar foods, behaviors, and even material items like the flag serve as affirmations of identity, security, and belonging. At funerals and memorial services across the nation and across creeds, familiar rituals and nurturing elements provide the clan with purpose, bonding, and impetus to move forward in life.

Though a funeral banquet is not exactly the same as eating in church, it is close, and one of the best comments I have ever encountered on that topic was written by Daniel Sacks, who stated, "Christians have been eating in church as least since the Last Supper; these meals have served a variety of purposes" (Sacks 2000: 62). Food, associated with one's religious center, is a part of the life of the congregation. There are many mores and folkways inherent in the religious and ethnic traditions of the American people, and they vary widely according to the representative group; however, as Charles Camp stated, for many the first dish offered for comfort at the death of someone's loved one is the casserole.[1]

Americans who offer casseroles as a comfort at the time of mourning may be unknowingly repeating a food tradition that has been popular for over three thousand years (or more). The early Romans "were also fond of casseroles, something taught them by the Greeks, and [also] pies filled with all sorts of things" (Smith 1989: 76). Contemporary Italian Americans and others with origins in the Mediterranean region often serve beans with their meals throughout the year as a matter of course. Yet Betty Fussell, regional foods expert, wrote that before the Spanish explorers returned from the Americas with their pockets full of beans and other seeds, fava beans were the only broad beans known in Europe (Fussell 1986: 50). Some classes of Romans (early Italians, of course), "believed that the souls of their ancestors resided in [fava] beans, so beans were eaten at funerals" (Duyff 1999:11). The upper-class Greeks and Romans, however, "had an ambivalent attitude to beans which some believed to contain the souls of the dead and others blamed for causing defective vision" (Tannahill 1989: 157).

The tradition of eating fava beans in Mediterranean cultures continues, but it is not necessarily attached to the ancient belief that their progenitors are residing in the beans. Jeff Smith wrote: "this is the strangest practice, but a practice loved by the Romans. When the fresh fava beans arrive in the springtime, people come to the market and purchase them, shell them, and eat them raw, some of them eating these right in the middle of the market. They dip them in a bit of salt and pepper mixed with olive oil" (Smith 1989: 422).

Church dinners and ethnic food events serve a variety of purposes, and eating either in the church or elsewhere as a community is a custom practiced by every group from American Indians and Asian

Americans to African Americans, Mexican Americans, and European Americans. Further, food beliefs, taboos, and rituals related to mourning and funerary celebrations have often become intercultural and reflect both synchronic and diachronic boundary crossings. Consider the funeral dinner of my husband's aunt held in her honor at an Italian restaurant. Neither she nor any of the family is Italian. That didn't matter. The dinner was more about pleasing everyone with popular Italian food than anything else. That she was Protestant, a nondrinker, and of English heritage really didn't make any difference.

Ancient European, Asian, and American food traditions and taboos, interesting yet largely forgotten, are nonetheless related to contemporary practices of mourning rituals associated with death. Our contemporary behaviors and traditions are often rooted in legacies from the past, and we perform them ritually without recognizing the origins. In this chapter, the discussion begins with a few of those old beliefs and practices and then turns to more recent developments in food and mourning practices in the contemporary United States.

Salt, Chopsticks, and Traditions

Many Americans enjoy foods with the flavor of China, Japan, and Indonesia. Eating the often salty food Asian-style has become common, and using chopsticks is popular in the United States among people who have never traveled in the Asian part of the world. Even my grandchildren (ages twelve, ten, eight, and five) have become adept at using them. In Japan, there are several taboos regarding the handling of chopsticks at the meal table. Some of these strong mandates are associated with the use of chopsticks in Buddhist funeral rites. According to Buddhist custom, after cremation, the bones and ashes are separated by mourners, who then pass the bone fragments from one set of chopsticks to another and place them in a columbarium. The fragments are collected in a specific order: legs, arms, hipbone, back bone, teeth, and skull, with the Adam's apple being retrieved last by a person who is the closest kin of the deceased. Because of this ancient practice, foods are not to be passed from one set of chopsticks at the table to another set of chopsticks. Further, chopsticks are never to be stuck upright in a bowl of rice at the meal table because that position denotes death. This position of the chopsticks is reserved for honoring the deceased. It is common to place the dead family member's own chopsticks upright in an offering bowl of uncooked rice positioned either at the family altar or beside the body of the deceased after it is prepared for viewing.

Salt—which carries many symbolic uses and meanings ranging from food preservation to a simple flavoring to a preserver of life—is used by many cultures in association with death, mourning, and rituals. One Japanese funerary tradition is to give a small packet of salt, as well as rice, sugar, onions, and garlic, to the Buddhist monks as they leave to return to their home or temple after a Japanese burial service. The gifts, which may also include a robe, are donated to the monks in thanksgiving for their presence and prayers on behalf of the deceased. Other guests are also sent away with a small sachet of salt, which is to be sprinkled in each corner of their home to drive away any evil that may be lurking. Sachets of salt are still passed out at contemporary Japanese funerals in the United States. The Buddhist Japanese also hold a traditional religious service seven days after a death and conduct a purification ceremony that involves the sprinkling of salt dissolved in water. Salt appears frequently in their various rituals.

During the mourning period in some Hindu sects, family members are to subsist entirely on sacrificial foods or foods donated by others for the period of mourning, and they are not to eat or use any mineral salt or ordinary salt in honor of the transition of the deceased. In Gaelic Ireland, in the nineteenth century, "watchers," that is, people attending a wake, "were expected to carry salt in their pockets, from which they ate from time to time. . . . [T]he use of salt may be thought in the circumstances to have been merely an encouragement to drink the liquors generously provided, but we find it constantly used for strictly ceremonial purposes in funeral rites" (Puckle 1926: 64).

One of the most unusual services performed for the dead was

that of the sin-eater. In the Irish tradition, the belief was that the sins of the deceased could be taken over by a sin-eater—someone willing to perform that ignoble role in return for a low fee and a scanty meal. The process, which took place outdoors, involved the corpse being placed on a bier, after which the sin-eater was to perch on top of the deceased and eat a loaf of bread to be washed down with a large basin of beer. The sin-eater was paid a sixpence (the pay might vary) for the vicarious assumption of the deceased's sins. The belief was that since the sin-eater now owned the sins of the deceased, the deceased would not be restless or walk after death. Some scholars suggest a connection between the sin-eater and the Jewish scapegoat of the Old Testament.

The symbolic use of salt as a ritual custom and even a signal of trust and hospitality has appeared in ancient records from around the world. The pre-Christian–era Celtic salt mines in Austria attest to the value of salt as an economic commodity many centuries ago. Ancient Egyptians used sodium chloride in mummification. The historian Herodotus recorded, almost two thousand years after the high Egyptian era (in gruesome detail), the importance of salt in the process of preparing the corpse after death. The Romans themselves served salt at their tables; in fact, "since salt symbolized the binding of an agreement, the absence of a saltcellar on a banquet table would have been interpreted as an unfriendly act and reason for suspicion" (Kurlansky 2002: 65). Salt has been used in ritual responses to life as well, including the Jewish tradition of using non-iodized, kosher salt for the Seder or Passover meal, a celebration of the Angels of Death who passed by ancient Jewish homes without inflicting harm. Because salt has been a necessary part of human survival, and a constant presence in one form or another, superstitions about its use and meaning can be expected. "Pass me salt, pass me sorrow," is an old saying from my own family. Another of my mother's warnings was, "If you spill the salt, you must throw some over your shoulder for good luck." There is a Jewish custom of sprinkling salt on bread for luck, and many Americans of Eastern European or Slavic descent continue to follow that custom. The earth provides the elements needed for human survival, and both in life and in death, salt has played a role in the lore and practice of the people.

Funeral Biscuits in Early America

The molasses cookies passed out to people attending funerals in parts of early America were so common as to have been nearly lost to history.[2] They were so common that mentioning them in a history would be like mentioning that the sky is often blue. Stamped with symbolic motifs (most commonly a heart), William Weaver called this simple token "edible folk art." Other symbols commonly pressed on these simple shortbread or "short gingerbread" biscuits might be "a cherub or winged head" (Weaver 1989: 118)—symbolizing the spirit of the deceased rising to heaven—"an hourglass, or even a skull" (Weaver 1989: 107). Because death was a frequent intruder in colonial life, larger cities even had bakeries that specialized in funeral cookies. This practice provided a connectedness between settlers of European descent in the early colonies.

The funeral biscuits were used among British and German Americans from Virginia's eastern shore to central Pennsylvania, and "the custom was so commonplace that it was hardly news in early letters and accounts" (Weaver 1989: 106). Served with wine in England and continental Europe, these hard molasses, ginger, and caraway flavored biscuits were meant to be dipped in beer, ale, or wine before eating. In Montgomery County, Pennsylvania, for instance, a prevailing funeral custom was that a young man and young woman would stand on either side of a path that led from the church house to the cemetery. The young woman held a tray of funeral biscuits and sweet cakes; the young man carried a tray of spirits and a cup. As mourners passed by, they received a sweet from the maiden and a sip of spirits from the cup furnished by the young man. A secular communion of sorts, these were ritual behaviors that transcended countries of origin and melded a diverse young nation with the common cords of death, mourning, and tradition. The funeral biscuit served as part of a code representing understood messages of mourning, honor, and remembrance.

Death, Mourning, and Foods in Nineteenth-Century America

In the 1800s, the deceased was usually washed, dressed, and laid out in the parlor of the house. The "visitors often engaged in a variety of activities, including somber reflection, scripture reading, [and] socializing, which usually involved some eating and drinking" (Laderman 1996: 31). The demeanor of the visitors varied with social and economic class and the culture and mores of the local community. In both rural and urban areas, food and drinks were shared. Familiar dishes of vegetables and fruit, meats and bread, cakes and pies were available to guests along with wine and punch. This sharing of time, simple foods, and conversation created a sense of community in spite of the loss of a valued member of the group. Neighbors and other acquaintances of all ages visited the home, paid their respects to the family and the deceased, partook of refreshments, and then went their way.[3] In nineteenth-century America, death was a common visitor to the community. Conversation, like conversation at funeral parlors today, ranged from politics to economic concerns to other timely news events.

Before the Civil War, funerals in the Northeast, specifically Boston, followed strict social and city customs and regulations. Laderman describes the male-dominated processions where women were allowed only very small roles in the "public acts surrounding the burial of the dead" (Laderman 1996: 48). Women of the upper-middle and upper classes were largely confined to their homes, where they guided servants in creating generous meals and comfortable surroundings. However, it was often the women who prepared the bodies of children and other women for viewing at the home wakes. Men prepared the men. The city regulations extended to racial separation, and blacks, for instance, were not allowed to use hearses. They were carried on the shoulders of friends and family to their burial places in specific areas of the cemetery outside of the space reserved for whites.

Less affluent households served more modest meals, but the custom was then, as it is now, to care for the bereaved by providing foods and relieving them from day-to-day responsibilities for varying periods of time.

As the United States saw immigration waves in 1848 and 1885, and with its change from chiefly an agrarian society to industrial nation, both the types of foods eaten in America as well as the style of serving them were strongly influenced by the European cultures of the immigrants. The Jews added rich dishes like cheesecake and noodles with creamed cheese as well as the now familiar bagels and chopped liver. The Irish added potato soup and soda bread; the Italians and Asians brought great varieties of noodles and pastas. Jeff Smith reminds us, "It is hard to think of a Polish meal without wonderful sausage. . . . Kielbasa, the simple Polish word for sausage" (Smith 1990: 403). We eat great varieties of foods today hardly contemplating their origins; they are all a part of our great, American cuisine. As stated earlier, Americans' move to the small apartments of urban landscapes led to the establishment of funeral parlors for viewings of the deceased, because of the lack of space in the home. Meals after the burial were often still held at home, however, and the fare was humble and reflective of the cultural traditions.

On the other hand, as time moved on after the Civil War, African Americans of the South conducted wakes, burials, and funeral banquets with a syncretic mix of traditions from Old World and New. There is a story in the text *Gumbo Ya Ya: Folk Tales of Louisiana* (Saxon et al. 1998: 301) that encapsulates the African American spirit concerning typical funerals in the later nineteenth and early twentieth centuries. It describes Crazah Louis, a veteran funeral attendee who frequented local black funerals to help himself to the food. His reputation of showing up at local funerals was nearly as sure as the presence of Death itself, the text tells us. The text also suggests that the description of Crazah may have been an exaggeration, but the gathering of people at funeral celebrations created a community of joy. "Negros [sic] prepare for dying all of their lives. As one of them put it, 'Moses died, Elijah died. All the strong men die and all the weak men die. There is no two ways about it, we all must die. So why not be ready for it, brother'" (Saxon et al. 1998: 310, 302).

The lively black funeral celebrations and foods will be discussed further in this chapter, but there is an observance in Georgia, and other states, that is thought to help meet the deceased person's spiri-

tual needs. It is the practice of placing on the grave broken bits of pottery and possessions last used by the dead person, "for the purpose of
supplying the needs of the spirit." Mason Brewer wrote that "the
spirit don't stay in the grave. When the funeral procession starts tuh
leave, the spirit leaves the body an' follows the people frum the graveyard. It nevuh stays with the body" (Brewer 1968: 307–8). I have
seen broken pottery placed on grave sites in black cemeteries in Missouri, Louisiana, and South Carolina. A continuing contemporary
practice, it evidences belief in the temporal needs of the deceased in
the afterlife.

Late Nineteenth Century and The Gilded Age

Mark Twain called the period following the Civil War (1870–1890)
"the Gilded Age" because he observed it to be golden and glittery only
on the surface. Huge corporations had been formed; it was the age of
the so-called Robber Barons—Rockefeller, Vanderbilt, Carnegie, Mor-
gan, and others. The promise of forty acres and a mule to every freed
black had not been fulfilled, and instead it was an age of broken promises, incredible influxes of immigrants (from the 1880s to 1920), and a
time when extreme poverty contrasted sharply with Victorian indul-
gence. Thorstein Veblen named the showy excess "conspicuous consumption,"[4] and that is what it appeared to be to most people. The
affluence of many in the 1980s was dubbed with the same phrase in
many minds. There are always individuals who make a show of wealth,
and as Veblen wrote in 1899, "Conspicuous consumption of valuable
goods is a means of reputability" (Veblen 1979: 75).

Upper-class cults, as Veblen referred to them, spared no expense
at the time of death. Elaborate caskets and floral arrangements, cas-
cades of black silk, and officious processions to remove the deceased
from home to a church and then to the cemetery for burial became
curious entertainments for bystanders. The funerary banquets following the burial were equally elaborate, for exotic and abundant
food was another demonstration of means. It was an age of commod-
ification, and success was often visually measured. Funerals, wakes,
and associated foods and drink ranged from the humble to the ex-

treme, and the funeral parlor became a common part of the urban landscape. Gary Laderman wrote that "Even as the corpse became a commodity in the new funeral industry and entered a complex network of commercial activity, it was represented as a potentially valuable object that imposed sacred obligations on the living" (Laderman 1996: 175).

For the people who could afford it, homes were built with bay windows large enough to provide space for a casket. The less affluent used the burgeoning mortuary business to accommodate their needs. In this late-nineteenth- and early-twentieth-century period, the funeral service was molded into an industry; it served the needs of the people, both rich and poor, and caring for the dead became a business throughout the United States.

Foods Associated with Contemporary Mourning in the United States

Most cultures in the United States have an after-meal when the funeral and burial or memorial service are completed. Across the many ethnic and religious groups that are represented here, however, there are both commonalities and differences. The Native American traditional response to death, for instance, is generally subdued and little conversation and conviviality take place after the burial or cremation. In interviews with both Native Americans and Anglo scholars of the North American Indian groups, I was told that to speak of the dead, or to mention their name, was behavior to be avoided. As far as typical foods following the Native American funeral celebration, the only thing that can be counted on is fry bread—a simple wheat dough sphere, fried lightly, and folded over, that is commonly used either plain or with vegetables and/or meat. For the traditional Native American, there is no funeral banquet; yet, there are many contemporary Native Americans who use mortuary services and follow standard funerary ritual practices in popular use.

From quiet, traditional Jewish and Islamic American practices regarding the time immediately following the services to the more lively Irish, Italian, Mexican, and African American post-funeral meals, to the large family gatherings of many other American groups—Greek Orthodox, Episcopal, Presbyterian, Methodist, Southern Baptist, Lutheran, and Mormon—the family feasts are times of both waning sorrow and emergent joy. They are reflected upon by most people I interviewed as times of reunion and renewed relationships. The deep sorrow of the separation by death is softened by the presence of close friends and family, and familiar foods evoke both memories and promising signals of the continued celebration of life.

The above discussion of salt as a food ingredient associated with death, both as a preservative and as a flavoring, leads to consideration of other common foods and perhaps uncommon ways they are used at the time of death. Honey, wheat, olive oil, wheat flour, eggs, nuts, olives, specific herbs and spices, coffee, tea, and often wines are commonly present in the funerary food customs of most of the cultures mentioned. The use of these simple, often comforting ingredients continues in many forms. Honey, for instance, one of the most ancient foods, has been used in a variety of ways since the Bronze Age. It has been used in the brewing of mead, a fermented alcoholic beverage common throughout the early world. For most of the groups mentioned above, beer, our contemporary version of mead, is a ubiquitous presence at family gatherings, including post-funeral reunions of those who imbibe. Honey and honeycomb, easily available sweets, have been enjoyed since antiquity. Beeswax has been used for embalming, sealing coffins, and, like salt, it has been used in the process of mummification. As was stated earlier, honey, considered a medicine by some Muslims and a food by others, is sometimes placed on the lips of the dying to provide comfort at the moment of death. Though Muslims are a part of nearly all of the countries and cultures of the world, honey flavored fruits and vegetables are particularly common to the table of Muslims from the Middle East, and their sweet presence offer a comforting familiarity at the after-meal.

In the Greek tradition, foods for the post-funeral banquet are prepared by Greek American women of the congregation using certain herbs and spices, and honey is used as a sweetener in a variety of ways. Charles Camp wrote that "cultural patterning of foodways may be found in the smallest details of events and customs . . . [such as] the characteristic use of cinnamon in Greek American cooking"(Camp 1989: 115). There are specific aromas that seem to permeate the hall where the Greek Orthodox people share the post-funeral meal. Traditional use of familiar herbs and spices loan a familiar and comforting atmosphere to the occasion. Though the dinner is varied in content, it usually includes familiar and traditional foods such as lamb, baked macaroni, *dolmanthes* (stuffed grape leaves), Greek breads, and perhaps cheese dishes such as *spanakopita* (spinach pie) or *tyropita* (Greek cheese pie), and *baklava*. Baklava, to the uninitiated, is a rich, layered phyllo pastry filled with nuts and saturated with honey. It is a sweet nearly always present at the finish of a Greek dinner.

Wheat flour is another ingredient found in the foods commonly associated with funerary food rituals. Besides traditional foods and tastes, there are intersections of foods and cultural practices. Two of the specific death-related foods in the Greek tradition are *kollyva* and *pazimadia*. Kollyva (or *koliva*) is a complex boiled wheat dish that contains sugar and currents in addition to basic flour, oil, spices, sesame seed, and walnuts. It is prepared in a large, shallow pan and finally enhanced with the shape of a cross before serving. It is shared at the end of the special service for departed souls called *mnemosinon* (memorial service) and "it is to recall to mind the departed soul, and [to remind] the bereaved to make a special appeal to pray . . . for his salvation. According to the Church tradition, koliva is offered in the Church three days, nine days, forty days, six months, one year after death, and whenever desired thereafter" (Karay and Nome 1985: 71). Present at this memorial meal is also a traditional walnut toast called pazimadia. Served as a side dish, it is more commonly known as zweiback, a mixture of wheat flour, eggs, spices, walnuts, and toasted sesame seeds.

In the Jewish tradition, a meal of condolence (*Seudat Havra'ah*) is served after returning from the cemetery. The meal is highly symbolic and based on a tradition from the Talmud that directs that the first meal after the burial must be served by friends and neighbors. "Indeed, the rabbis of the Jerusalem Talmud admonished neighbors who left the bereaved to prepare their own meal. They even pronounced a curse upon such people for displaying callousness and indifference to the plight of their fellow men" (Lamm 2000: 94). The belief is that the bereaved may be feeling so deeply distressed that life has lost its meaning. They may feel that eating is of no use. Therefore, this meal of condolence, provided by the closest friends, provides more than simple sustenance; it both symbolizes and provides a formal expression of caring and consolation. If the mourner is ready to talk about his or her feelings, or has reflections about the deceased, the meal of condolence also provides sympathetic listeners with whom to share the moments.

The Seudat Havra'ah is usually a dairy meal and includes no meat. The first meal is primarily made up of foods considered symbolic of life: lentils, peas, eggs, and round rolls and bagels. A second traditional explanation is that "round and oval foods, particularly eggs, are served at the meal of condolence because they have no mouth, that is, they have no opening. They represent the mourner, still in shock, who has no words for anyone" (Baba Batra 16b [qtd. in Kolatch 1996: 194]). The eggs are hard-cooked symbolizing the necessity of strength and endurance. The roundness of the eggs also represents the wheel of life and ever-revolving change—from joy to sadness and returning to joy again. Bagels, round and easily digested, are also often served at this meal. "Because of their shape—with no beginning and no end—bagels symbolize the eternal cycle of life. In the old days, they were supposed to be a protection against demons and evil spirits, warding off the evil eye and bringing good luck. For this reason, they were served at circumcisions and when a woman was in labor and also at funerals, along with hard boiled eggs" (Roden 1999: 100).

During the early weeks of mourning, family, friends and relatives continue to provide the bereaved family with various foods, many of which represent familiar tastes and shared remembrances. Food carries complex messages in all cultures, and because of the scarcity of food that Jews have experienced many times in their history, "food represents a mother's love—and that was one thing the Jews did not lack. The Yiddisheh mammeh manifested her unbreakable and unconditional love by constant and solicitous overfeeding" (Roden 1999: 43). Anthropologist Karen Brodkin's book about Jewish life in America fondly recalls her grandmother's model of Jewish womanhood, and the messages she sent through food. It also provides a segue to a discussion of Italian food responses at the time of death. Brodkin wrote: "My grandmother's work identity came out full force in cooking. She took total charge of the kitchen, and meals were high in labor and calories: handmade noodles, rendered chicken fat, matzo balls, split pea soup, blintzes, kugel, potato latkes, gefilte fish . . . Everything from scratch. . . . As with most of the Jewish and Italian families I knew, love was tied up with food" (Brodkin 2000: 16). Rather than verbalize affection, feelings were often demonstrated by behaviors believed by many cultures to thwart the destroyer of happiness—the evil eye, a name given to a piercing gaze or stare thought to have the ability to focus negative energy and bad luck on the victim because of envy. By honoring the family of the deceased with the time-intensive labor of preparing and presenting wholesome foods, both traditional and familiar, the bonding love and support of the community is again expressed and familiar codes reaffirmed.

Like the Jews, many first-, second-, and third-generation Italians also believe in protecting themselves and their families from the evil eye. *Cornicelli,* "little red horns," appear to be much like a red pepper, and are amulets sometimes hung over the doorway or near the bed of the very ill or dying in the belief that the cornicelli will ward off bad luck and evil spirits. These good luck charms represent natural or manmade weapons (like teeth, claws, or horns) that fight off evil. Another protection against evil by use of a common food is found, for many Italians, in the efficacy of grain sprouts. Those grown in the dark in the consecrated ground of a churchyard or a crypt, are believed to "protect against Satan and the forces of chaos" (Gambino 1975: n.p.).

In *Growing Up and Growing Old in Italian-American Families,* Colleen Leahy Johnson revealed many cultural folkways and mores in her description of the post-funeral Italian meal. Ideally, the meal is to be prepared and served in the home because meals held in restaurants (or even catered in the home) reflect a lack of family community or of helping each other in a time of need. The expediency of restaurant food or caterers reflects "the American way of doing things," rather than the traditional Italian way, and having an "American" wife may prevent even an Italian son from having the wake or post-funeral meal in their home because it might be said, "she never got into the Italian way" (Johnson 1985: 99). "Getting into the Italian way" means providing a profuse array of tasty dishes. One respondent remembering this even in his childhood concluded, "Death never scares me. It has always seemed like a big neighborhood social" (Johnson 1985: 99).

Food preparation and sharing are ritualistic and ceremonial in the Italian culture. In a sense, they are a type of communion between family members. The structure and performance of a funeral meal are required to be presented in "the Italian way," a fixed and expected manner rather than a dynamic process. Italian American mothers, not unlike the often-spoken-of Jewish mothers (or dedicated mothers of any culture), demonstrate their affection by providing family and friends of the deceased with the staple foods: eggplant parmigiana, breaded veal, spaghetti, lasagna, chicken prepared with various sauces, ravioli, pasta with pesto, baked ziti, and manicotti. Vegetables, fresh fruit, and beans are commonly served, and also fish and fine cheeses. Coffee, and a variety of wines, often in gallon-sized jugs, are enjoyed, and any or all of these foods (and many more) would be provided for the family both at the time of death and at the post-funeral meal. The common ingredients of olive oil, olives, wheat products, specific herbs and spices, favorite meats, and other elements mentioned above are used in ways unique to the Italian culture. Cuisine is considered a crowning achievement of Italy, and to Italian Americans, each meal is significant. The enormous variety of foods represent regional specialities and are legacies from Florence, Venice, Genoa, Piedmont, Rome, Naples, and other areas in the north and south of Italy. The bereaved family is surrounded by familiar faces and wished well by carefully and traditionally prepared and served foods and beverages.

In the Old Country, it is not unusual for the women to prepare and serve foods to male mourners who are seated together at long tables. William Grant, retired now after serving as longtime chair of the American Culture Studies Program at Bowling Green State University, described a funeral feast he attended in Southern Italy. The food was prepared in a small restaurant by the women, and the men were seated outside at a long, cloth-covered table. There were no women included in this post-funeral meal. Professor Grant said that he had never seen (or enjoyed) such a variety of foods, including ham, pastas, plates of antipasto, and not only wine but fine whiskey (Grant, personal interview, June 22, 2003).

Southern Funeral Foods, Black and White

Early days of slavery and suffering have thankfully long-passed for black Americans in the United States, but often their family foods shared on gathering occasions still carry the influences and traditions of the Deep South. Dorothy Height wrote that "soul food is fondly described as 'food made with feeling and care.' It evolved from the rich heritage of African customs, was shaped by Southern cookery practices, expanded by similarly tribal habits of Native Americans, and regionally influenced by West Indian, Caribbean and French cooking" (Height 1994: 200).

Again, most of the same ingredients—salt, honey, nuts, wheat, sugar, specific herbs and spices, potatoes, chicken, pork, vegetables, and fruits—are used to create the familiar tastes of African American culture. The tradition of taking food to the bereaved family continues as a community and familial ritual. Karla F.C. Holloway suggests that traditional fried chicken taken to the family these days may be from Kentucky Fried Chicken instead of having been prepared in a family kitchen, but the ongoing practice of "providing meals to a grieving family cycles through the entire bereavement process for black folk, starting with the wake and concluding with a formal meal after the funeral services" (Holloway 2002: 166).

Windsor Jordan, of Mary Jordan's Catering Service in Atlanta, Georgia, described a modern, catered version of the church meal. At the time of death, the bereaved are emotionally and physically exhausted, so they are given "a solid menu: barbecued ribs, hot catfish, fresh pork ham, *baked* chicken [not fried—this is, after all, a "ca-tered" affair], turnip greens, pasta salad, mushrooms, sweet potato pie, and cheesecake." Jordan alluded to a gospel song whose lyrics talk of going to heaven "in golden shoes and high-heeled slippers with angels singing," but he said his clients don't wait for that: they "start [celebrating] here on earth" (Patureau 1995: D2 [qtd. in Hol-loway 2002: 167]).

In *The Black Family Reunion Cookbook: Recipes and Memo-ries,* Jessica B. Harris discusses some of the characteristics of African American foods representative of those served anytime there are fam-ily gatherings. Gathering around the table for long, lingering meals and talk is an old black American tradition, and Harris describes the mingling of foods and cultures:

> The old adage has it that you are what you eat. If that's true, Black Americans are made up of a multiplicity of wonderful things. We're comprised of a dash of cornbread, a hint of chitlins, a rounded table-spoon of biscuit dough, a good measure of molasses and a seasoning of fatback. To the mix are added such regional flavorings as a bit of benne from Charleston, South Carolina, and a hint of praline from New Orleans. There's a dash of catfish and a pinch of dandelion wine. The recipe is ever-changing with new tastes being brought from "cousins" from Africa and the Caribbean. We're baked, roasted, fried, and sautéed and the result has yielded us in all colors of the rainbow from lightly toasted to a deep well done. It's not at all sur-prising then that we have developed a language and a vocabulary of food that is uniquely ours . . . whether it's savored on the edge of a wooden spoon straight from a cast iron cauldron or served on heir-loom china on a hand crocheted tablecloth, it is all a part of what makes us us. (National Council of Negro Women 1993: 197)

Like the African American range of food styles, from casual to elegant, simple to gourmet, the foods of both southern and northern white folks fall into a spectrum of familiar and typical American family foods with regional influences. Neighbors and friends furnish foods for the bereaved family as soon as the news is received, and typical dishes taken to the home are similar to the foods taken to tra-ditional potluck dinners at the many churches. Baptists, Methodists, Lutherans, Presbyterians, Congregationalists, Episcopalians, and other Christian groups, in spite of somewhat differing religious perspectives and philosophies, have similar responses to the meaning of foods at the time of death. Spirit-nurturing recipes of varied casseroles, deviled eggs, coleslaw, Jell-O salads, macaroni salads, and potato salads are nearly always present in the food offerings to the family and at the dinners served at the church after traditional funerals and burial. Southern fried chicken (hot and cold), sliced hams and roasts, corn breads and muffins, other breads, cakes, pies, and plates of cookies are prepared in individual homes and taken promptly to either the home of the bereaved, or to the church for the after-funeral meal. At the church, the food is usually served buffet style with family and close friends. Sometimes this same type of buffet takes place in the home after the interment. Some Christian religions have strict prohibitions against liquor of any kind, and in those homes or churches, fruit punch, iced water or tea, and hot coffee are served. Otherwise, wine, beer, and mixed drinks are usually available even when the dinner is held in the church hall or parish house. Again, some families use banquet halls in restaurants or simply gather at tables at a restaurant.

Another variety of foods, the so-called White Trash cooking, given that name because the cooking involves common, inexpensive ingredients (often home-produced), is alive and well in the rural South. In the Bible Belt, though not everyone belongs to any one, single faith, the cooking traditions are popular and widespread and the dominant religion is Southern Baptist. Perlow, a sausage, tomato, and rice dish with tomatoes, green peppers, and hot seasonings, is just one of the well-known and popular recipes served at gatherings of family and friends in this region, and it often shows up at funeral feasts. "If you live in the South or have visited there lately, you know that the old White Trash tradition of cooking is still very much alive, especially in the country" (Mickler 1986: 3). Except for in the region near the southern coast, this tradition of cooking is less spicy and quite different from traditional soul food. There is great variety in the food, which ranges from old standbys like banana pudding and whiskey pie to fried oysters and watermelon preserves. Cabbage salads, dark green vegetables, dumplings, deviled eggs, fruit salads, ham, hot dogs, and even potato/peanut butter candy continue to be prepared and shared in this regional style. The "White Trash" label, more a southern joke than a pejorative term, when applied to food, suggests simple to prepare, often high-sugar/high-fat foods. In contrast to the carefully prepared typical Southern cuisine, "White Trash" cooking is quick, inexpensive, and often not good for you.

Various foods are packed and taken to cemeteries now and then to provide a picnic feast for family members who clean and care for the grave sites. This is a common practice both in the South and in the West, where cemeteries are often in need of care. With rising numbers of people interested in roots and genealogy, the visits to the cemetery also afford a time for checking dates and spellings and photographing family plots. According to the region of the country, traditional picnic foods are packed and enjoyed. In the South, the family might pack fried chicken and potato salad; on the West Coast, the picnic foods might be light salads, fruit, bread, and cheese; on Michigan's Upper Peninsula (U.P.), a family might take a pasty and fruit for family members. Family stories emerge from these visits, which reflect the importance and constancy of community and humor in the family outings. Again, we see the ubiquitous presence of the same basic ingredients flavored and interpreted with love and regional or cultural influences.

Native American Mourning Rituals

For thousands of years, in all parts of the Western Hemisphere, Native Americans have lived and practiced their own belief systems and rituals—even, in more recent times, in spite of the tremendous odds European and Asian colonization has placed against them. Old practices have often been lost and revived or reinvented, and the customs concerning death, burial, or cremation and the use of certain foods for funerary ritual are as varied as the hundreds of officially registered tribes still struggling to survive in the United States. The following funerary food traditions among the Native Americans carry deep symbolism. Just as Native American stories are layered with meaning—some meant to be heard on the level of entertainment, some for instruction, and some with sacred implications—the foods too have layered meanings.

Most Native American people believe that death is simply the beginning of a journey into another place. The living feel responsible to ensure the departed a good start, and some tribes, the Potawatomi for instance, have a funeral feast and set a place for the deceased spirit. In that way, the spirit can share the food in a spiritual sense. In the Navajo tradition, foods may or may not be served after the funeral and/or burial. Should a dinner be served, corn is usually present because it is a mainstay of the Navajo diet. Mutton stew is the most typical Navajo main dish, and the fry bread (*Dah díníukggaazh*) is a very common food for many Native American people as discussed earlier. "[It] is served at parties, cookouts, and powwows as kind of a native 'soul food'" (Toelken 1996: 45). Fry bread is thought to have become a staple in the Navajo diet during their imprisonment at Fort Sumner. It is made with white flour, baking powder, salt, water, and lard. Shaped into a ball and then flattened, it is then fried in hot oil. According to preference, it is sometimes eaten with honey and sometimes eaten with salt.[5]

Because many of the tribes believe in the power of the living to influence the welfare of the deceased, there are many taboos concerning what kind of activities bereaved relatives may or may not engage in for a period of time after the death of a loved one. In some tribal practices, portions of the post-burial meal are set aside before the meal to honor and remember spirit ancestors. Some tribes believe that prolonged grieving can prevent the spirit of the deceased from crossing over to the next world, and it is also believed that the dead person should not be touched except by those directly involved in the body's preparation and burial. Further, many tribes believe that the name of the deceased should not be spoken because that too may delay the spirit's journey to the other world. Ceremonial dancing and even dressing in regalia is forbidden for a year after a death in some tribes. To them, restricting various behaviors represents an effort to make sacred through sacrifice the journey of their departed loved one. To provide this sacrifice among the living on behalf of the dead frees the living to continue to live in peace and harmony.

Mexican American Mourning Rituals

Mexican Americans have brought the varied food traditions of Mexico with them to the United States. Often what appear to be very simple dishes are difficult and time-consuming to prepare. Making some of the difficult dishes and giving them to the bereaved family is a demonstration by friends and extended family of caring and commitment. A typical food that may be served at a family gathering related to the death of a family member is hot, homemade chicken soup with flour tortillas. Coffee is plentiful and kept hot, and the convivial atmosphere sometimes takes on the air of a fiesta rather than a wake. Hot chocolate with cinnamon is usually prepared and served to children and others who would enjoy it.

Corn, chilies, tomatoes, and beans formed the basis of the indigenous Mexican kitchen and are still central to the diet of most Mexican Americans today. During the period of the wake, and for an undefined time afterward, foods are prepared and served in the bereaved's home by family members. The most traditional dish is tortillas with *carne* (meat) and tomatoes. A traditional dish, *menudo* (a tripe and vegetable soup), is often prepared and offered, but many contemporary Mexican Americans decline. Making tamales, steamed corn masa traditionally filled with a savory mélange of spices and shredded pork, serves as a way to bring people together as cooks. Working together on the tamales provides a time to talk, share memories, and simply enjoy being together.

There are many foods traditionally associated with the celebration of All Saints' Day and All Souls' Day on November 1 and 2, though many of the dishes are also served at other times of the year. *Pan de Muertos* (Bread of the Dead), a rich coffee cake, often carried to the grave site and left there, is decorated in many ways. Sometimes there is "a cross made of pieces of baked dough in the form of alternating teardrops and bones with a knob in the center" (Ortiz 1965: 288), and sometimes it is decorated with meringues shaped to look like bones. Though usually round, the cake itself may be shaped like a skull, and skull-shaped candies and papier-mâché skeletons may be added for further decoration. Pink or red icing or sprinkles or both are sometimes added to create an eerie note.

On All Souls' Eve, the continuing tradition carried to the United States from villages in Mexico is to place favorite food and drink for the dead, often including tamales and tequila, at the graveside in remembrance of the departed one. The next day, families usually have a feast of tamales and other typical Mexican foods served with coffee, beer, tequila, and followed with Pan de Muertos and sometimes skull-shaped cookies decorated with the names of family members.

Funerary Foods of Rapidly Growing American Groups

America, a dynamic and constantly changing society, continues to increase in diversity and cultural wealth. Since the middle of the twentieth century, ethnic groups that had been present in small numbers for centuries in the United States have been growing in size because of less-restrictive immigration laws. The multitude of cultures and belief systems in the United States prevents thorough discussion of the beautiful rituals and meaningful food traditions that are practiced in each, but those of the larger groups are presented here. There are commonalities and differences, but the concept of food traditions at the time of mourning consistently contributes to ongoing life. Muslim, Hindu, Buddhist, Tao, and Mormon food customs share many of the common ingredients mentioned earlier in the chapter. Certainly salt and honey play a part in their food ways, as well as various vegetables, fruits, meats and fish, grains, nuts, oils, and dairy products. All of these groups have a traditional funeral feast after the closure of the funeral and cremation or interment of the deceased. The Muslim and Mormon families and friends usually return to their worship center for a meal that has been prepared by women of the congregation. The Hindus, Buddhists, and Taoists sometimes retire to their homes for a meal but most commonly go to a banquet hall or restaurant for the after-meal.

Mansa Cargo, a Muslim woman who shared information about her congregational practices, reminds us that diversity is widespread among the Muslim people. Ms. Cargo wrote that "just in our Friday prayer, over forty nationalities were represented. Just in our women's meeting, attended by 20 women, I would say [there were] ten nationalities, at least" (Cargo, e-mail, February 9, 2004). The foods represented in this discussion are influenced by Middle Eastern culture, but it is important to remember that only 20 percent of Muslims are actually Middle Easterners, despite the common misconception that most Muslims are from that region. Comforting and aiding a mourning Muslim family with foods that need no preparation or attention other than heating before serving is a traditional obligation of the Muslim community. For two to three days, the family is to rest and begin to adjust to the change in their lives. It is a time for them to be supported and nourished emotionally and physically. Friends and relatives of the family often take gifts of fruit, desserts, and a variety of well-loved dishes according to the foods common to the family and their culinary roots. On the other hand, Cargo wrote that "some cultures instead, cook and feed all those who come to give their condolences. Others offer food after people come to the Mosque to read from the Koran. I personally might make a dinner for a close friend who might have lost a loved one" (Cargo, e-mail February 9, 2004).

Soups accompanied by bread may be given to the mourning family, as well as vegetable casseroles and lamb dishes. Other food gifts may include fruit, pastry treats such as baklava, cheese-filled pastries, or milk puddings prepared with a wide range of flavorings and ingredients. The most well-known food associated with Muslim funerary ritual is halma or helva, a funeral sweetmeat that is fragrant and has a rich, almost comforting taste. Because of its fragrance, this food is sometimes prepared at the home of the deceased after a funeral, where it is shared with visitors and neighbors. Recipes for this sweet vary, but the main ingredients are pine nuts, walnuts, sesame seeds, honey, flour, semolina (a coarse wheat flour left over after sifting), and butter or margarine. Three less well-known ingredients, mahleb (almond-flavored spice gleaned from the dark kernels inside the pits of small black cherries which grow wild), sultanas (small, yellow, seedless raisins), and pekmez (grape or mulberry molasses) are sometimes included. These less-familiar ingredients can usually be found in Turkish or Middle Eastern food shops. Claudia Roden, an international food writer, stated that the presentation of typical Middle Eastern food, down to the "humblest sauce or soup with a dusting of red paprika or brown cumin and a sprinkling of chopped parsley is the result of love and beauty and ornamentation" (Roden 2001: 10). When a family is mourning, simple but beautiful gifts and dishes are given to them with love and friendship to remind them that they are cared for and others sorrow for them. Lauri Patel, a Muslim woman, said: "The food represents caring. It is cultural, and is often prepared with influence from the nation of origin, but not always. People taking the food will try to prepare what the family likes, and the foods taken also depend on the region [from which the family comes]" (Patel, telephone interview, February 9, 2004).

Mormon Funerary Foods

In *Memories That Live: Utah County Centennial History,* a mid-twentieth-century post-funeral meal is described in this way: "After everything was finished, the mourners returned to their home where they would find a hot meal awaiting them, prepared by the same kind friends and neighbors who had helped throughout all of the few sad difficult days" (Huff 1947: 109). Today, this tradition continues in contemporary Utah practice, but the after-funeral banquet is usually held in the cultural hall of the church. The news of a death in the ward passes through a network of friends and associates quickly, and the women of the congregation are prompt in providing comforting foods for the bereaved family. This custom has continued for so many decades and is considered so integral to the fellowship given in these tightly knit communities, that it is simply an expectation of most women to be called upon to provide this service. Many different kinds of foods will be taken to the family, though there is no particular regional food expected. The variety of casseroles, vegetable dishes, salads, Jell-O variants, homemade breads, cakes, pies, and cookies are generous and almost endless.

In many parts of Utah, the traditional meal served at the ward house hall after the funeral is standardized. Though there are variants, the basic meal is ham; a recipe of scalloped or casseroled, cheese-flavored "funeral potatoes"; a tossed green salad, a Jell-O salad (usually green); rolls; and cookies, pie, or cake. One of the women I interviewed said that if we didn't serve the traditional meal, "the proper meal," when it was her turn, she would come back and haunt us all (Sutcher, personal interview, November 10, 2001).

The Oak Hills Stake in Provo, Utah, has prepared a guideline booklet for their membership based on *The Relief Society Action Manual.* (The Relief Society is a charitable organization for Mormon women.) It is designed to assist the Relief Society sisters in giving consistent, compassionate service. In the booklet are listed three "Menu Ideas for Funeral Luncheons." After interviewing several women from various wards and stakes in Utah County, I have determined that these are typical of the menus served in the Utah County area, but not in all of the state. The first is as listed above. The second ("nice for spring or summer"), is made up of ham sandwiches, potluck salads, baked beans or vegetables, and cake. The third menu is a "Box lunch for the road." This is used when the interment is out of town, or if families must leave immediately after the funeral service. It consists of ham sandwiches or fried chicken, sliced raw vegetables, a bag of potato chips, a cookie or brownie, a small carton of milk or juice, and a napkin (*Relief Society Action Manual* 1996: 11).

The deeply rooted relationships that are established in the Latter-day Saint wards are much like those in an old, Roman Catholic parish. Though the ward population is determined numerically, it may be made up of members who are widely scattered in a specific geographic area. Some may live as far as fifty or more miles apart. Or, particularly in Utah, the ward may be made up of only three or four blocks of families. Either way, the ward becomes a bonded village of sorts, and the members of the ward become much like extended family. Interaction takes place during a three-hour block of services on Sunday, on weekly or monthly temple trips, and in meetings sometimes scheduled during the week. In a religion where much of the teaching focuses on service and person-to-person responsibility, members become intensely entwined in one another's triumphs and tragedies. At a time of sorrow from prolonged illness or death in the

family, ward members rally and do their best to provide sustenance
and comfort to the bereaved without becoming invasive.

Indo-American Mourning Foods

Seldom is a traditional Asian Indian home without a courtyard for
growing herbs and other plants. Used for medicinal purposes and
ritual use, many Indo-Americans have adapted their American apartments, homes, and yards and invented ways to continue to produce
the plants they need. There are regional flavors carried from the many
cities and villages of their homeland, and the traditions concerning
foods are ancient and sacred to many Indo-Americans.

For this group, cremation marks the usual closure of the funeral
period. Family members gather to oversee the cremation at the cre-
matorium and then return to their homes for an eleven- or twelve-day
period of isolation. Traditional Hindus avoid partaking of salt, some
vegetables, and any meat during this time, and some families dress in
white during this period. While the family is in isolation, many foods
will be brought to them by friends and extended family. The insight-
ful Indo-Indian scholar K.T. Achaya, stated: "Food in the Aryan belief was not simply a means of bodily sustenance it was part of a
cosmic moral cycle" (Achaya 1994: 61). Because of belief in reincarnation, the Hindu tradition considers various aspects of the foods
that are used. Seasonings such as garlic and onion may create bodily
odors that may interfere and offend both humans and other living
creatures and create disharmony. It is believed that foods must be
carefully selected because they influence physical well-being as well
as mental and emotional makeup. Typical American foods that the
family would enjoy may be provided in addition to traditional dishes
representing symbolic foods and flavors. Though not all Hindus are
vegetarians, many are. Favored traditional foods would probably include milk and cheese dishes, vegetables and pulses such as lentils
and beans. Rice dishes are also popular. Popular traditional dishes
are curried chicken, tamarind chicken, various curries, tofu, and
mixed vegetable dishes such as green peas with lentils, chickpea potatoes, and eggplant tofu.

In some Hindu traditions, favorite foods of the deceased are served to the relatives on the third, fifth, seventh, and ninth days after the death. A photograph of the deceased may be displayed, and food is placed before it. Traditional Hindus in the United States carry with them deep cultural meanings, traditions, and beliefs about food taken from their homelands. There are many subsets to the Hindu cultural practices, but in all of them, food is handled, prepared, and eaten keeping in mind various observations of manners, customs, traditions, and taboos. Local and pervasive customs remove some foods from the diet, and these prohibitions vary greatly from region to region. Some foods that may be highly valued by one group may be held in disdain by another. For individuals from the Saurashtra region, "fish, flesh, fowl, and eggs are taboo practically everywhere. The Christian pork is a delicacy, to a Muslim it is anathema. . . . Diet variations were wide and were most based on factors which included availability of foodstuffs, religious and customary inhibitions and even personal prejudices (Noble and Dutt 1982: 291, 292).

It is believed by traditional Hindus that "in the great Aryan cosmic cycle, the eater, the food he eats, and the universe must all be in harmony" (Achaya 1994: 61). Because there are so many regions in India, each with its traditions and taboos, the following discussion of foods and customs can only be presented in a general way. Achaya suggests that "every community that lives in India has a distinct food ethos. Most of these, however, have been influenced by Aryan beliefs and practices" (Achaya 1994: 69). Because of the oppressive heat in India, cleanliness and the avoidance of pollution was important. Food cooking and eating practices were strictly followed, and those boundaries are still maintained by many in the United States. For instance, a cook or housewife was never to taste food during its preparation for fear of contamination. It was considered bad luck. Foods are classified as pure or impure, though the practice of these designations has become blurred. Because of the many boundaries and taboos associated with cleanliness, death became a traumatic event for a family. All eating and drinking would stop until the cremation was over. Then, during the mourning period, the frying of spices could not be undertaken, and relatives would provide the food for the family. Forbidden foods, usually welcome in the normal diet like milk and milk products, lentils, and turmeric, were to be entirely avoided during the mourning period. After a death, the cooking hearth might also be destroyed and replaced with a new one following the mourning period.

A typical Asian-Indian meal consists of about five or six dishes. In preparation of the foods, innovation and experimentation is encouraged, and experienced cooks of this cuisine seldom agree about the preparation of a particular dish. Sweets can be served at anytime during a meal, and usually both rice and a type of bread are served. There are rules for eating properly in the Indian tradition, and pieces of the bread are used with three fingers to scoop up the food in small bites. A family might have many different kinds of meats, fish, or vegetables brought in to them. Curry, ginger, garlic, coconut, cardamom, cinnamon, saffron, and chilies are favorite flavors, but the quantity and variety of spices, herbs, and other ingredients are left to the discretion of the cook. Many spices are used, but they are not necessarily hot to the taste. Foods taken into Indo-American homes at the time of bereavement may range from simply fruits and nuts to regional American favorites, to traditional foods from their homeland according to the family and its beliefs and tastes.

The preceding discussion of Indo-Americans' funerary foods, along with the following two sections on Chinese American and Japanese American foods and funerary customs, deserve to be contextualized. The three cultures are diverse within themselves, but overall they have distinct commonalities. The belief systems of the Indian, Chinese, and Japanese mythological and religious traditions are similar in their regard to human identity. The human state, or the self (both the body and the mind), is believed to be a transitory experience; additionally, all three traditions hold that a phenomenal essence or objective consciousness exists within each human, and it is believed to be intuitive. The belief is that the phenomenal essence is a pure and eternal phenomenon, and in most individuals, tremendous effort has to be made to put oneself in touch with that part of one's eternal makeup.

Taboos on foods and behaviors, the many restrictions culturally imposed on believers, and required homage to the ancestors and other practices are intended to help individuals remain in contact with the dead, purify their own and their ancestors' souls and bodies, and find the way, philosophically and physically, to rediscovery and contact with the eternal essence of self. In these belief systems, Hindu, Buddhist, and Taoist, the most important and fundamental quest is to examine, evaluate, and define one's life in the world at the moment in which one finds himself or herself.

The patterns, myths, philosophies, and cosmologies of these belief systems wind into the dim corridors of Asian antiquity. These three primary Indo-Asian religions are braided and woven in complex, overlapping patterns far beyond the scope of this text to isolate and explicate. But it is safe to say that Hinduism informed Buddhism, and Buddhism has been blended with Taoism to the point that it is hard to put crisp boundaries around either. Basically, there are the Hindu *Upanishads,* which furnish the philosophical doctrines, the *Vedas,* which contain the worldview and interrelationships within the universe, and many other Hindu philosophical and didactic writings including epic poems and stories. The story of Siddhartha Gautama Buddha is depicted in third- and fourth-century texts such as the *Mahivastu* and the *Lalitavistara.* Buddhism has legends and mystical elements, and it was adapted and blended with Taoism, essentially an ancient system that interpreted the way to establish communication between heaven and earth. Today, Hinduism has many sects. Buddhism and Taoism were influenced by Confucian ideology but also resisted its rule-bound tenets. Throughout the United States there are temples, gardens, cemeteries, and cemetery sections to accommodate the rich and complex beliefs and needs of Americans who follow these belief systems; and there are myriad restaurants and cooking guides easily available so that we can enjoy the rich aromas and tastes of their sumptuous cultures.

Chinese American Mourning Foods

In Chinese American custom, after the funeral there is a large dinner banquet for the family and close friends. In the United States, this is usually held at a Chinese restaurant. Many restaurants provide a preplanned, vegetarian menu, and it is sometimes listed on the menu as the post-funeral meal. Wine is served and taken with the meal. In the United States, this is frequently American or French wine because of the difficulty in obtaining Chinese wine. It is to be taken in moderation, and it is said that too much wine defeats the purpose of the carefully prepared food. An abundance of tea is a traditional part of the menu. Chopsticks are available because many Chinese Americans will use chopsticks at this meal and others. The nonviolent Confucius, some legends say, influenced the invention of chopsticks because he wanted to eliminate knives, a tool of power and war, from the tranquil dinner table.

Dim sum is a fried or steamed dumpling with a variety of fillings. A common finger food, it may be filled with vegetables, a sweet cream mixture, or a variety of meats or meat and vegetable combinations. It is served at traditional Chinese American dinners in the United States, and is a consistent and popular presence at Chinese American buffets. Soups are a traditional food for the Chinese, and many Chinese Americans have grown up on endless varieties of miso soup. The miso base or paste is created from rice, fermented barley, or soybeans. It many have vegetables and/or noodles added to it, and even the layering of ingredients in miso soup can carry traditional meaning. At a funeral banquet no fish or meat would be served in the soup, but commonly, miso may have fish, chicken, pork, or other meats added.

Many dishes, including rice, will be served to the family, and in many Chinese American restaurants, the food is placed on a revolving tray in the center of the table to provide easy access to the bowls of food. The Chinese and Chinese Americans do not believe that an exaggerated exhibition of sorrow is appropriate after the funeral. Having appropriately provided for the well-being of the deceased, the family enjoys the good fortune of plenty to eat in the presence and company of their loved ones.

Japanese American Funerary Foods

When examining the foods that Japanese Americans may associate with mourning, it is important to note that Japanese food traditions and practices in the United States differ significantly from those in Japan. Japan is a country of many villages and hamlets in addition to the large cities. There are regional flavors and ingredients there that are not available here. Though the Japanese people have been in the United States for over a hundred years, and have cultivated gardens to produce favorite vegetables and fruits, they have, overall, adapted their foods to regional availability. At the same time, they have maintained traditional tastes and also reinvented familiar recipes to please Americanized palettes.

Counting the days after death and performing certain rites on certain days has become relaxed in Japanese American culture. Traditionally, the first seven days after the death are days of abstinence. Only a small amount of food is used, and it is to be vegetarian. On the seventh day after death, called *sho-nanoka*, a feast of fish and wine would celebrate the end of abstinence. But, because of the loosening of traditions in the United States, the feast may take place on the same day as the funeral. People travel long distances to attend the ceremonies for the dead, and it is often too difficult to keep the ceremonies on the traditional days.

The foods of the Japanese appear to be simple, but many of them take long hours of preparation. In the Japanese American celebrations of Obon, a celebration in honor of the dead of a family, the foods are adapted for Japanese Americans and their many non-Asian guests. "The food sold in booths surrounding the Obon arena . . . is distinctly Japanese, but it is also designed to be palatable to a broad range of onlookers; the focus is on rice, teriyaki chicken, noodles, and sushi (vinegared rice and other ingredients rolled in a sheet of dried sea algae called nori) and not on raw fish, eel, or octopus, which are thought to be too exotic for the tastes of the general public" (Toelken 1994: n.p.). The Obon food at American celebrations, though distinctly representing a Japanese style, is prepared and flavored in a way that will appeal to the non-Japanese community. It not only feeds the interethnic community, but it also represents to non-Japanese a dimension of Japanese American family and home life.

From Japanese sushi and Native American fry bread to the funeral ham and traditional soda bread of the Irish, or the rich curries and chutneys of India, cherished recipes carry deep cultural meanings. The familiar foods evoke nostalgic memories and unassumingly proffer familiar grounding during the fragile and emotional time of mourning. These often simple but traditional ingredients of the world's kitchens appear in different combinations and shapes, with myriad aromas and fragrances refined over centuries of experiment and practice. These tempting foods, cultural markers, awaken in the mourning the will to continue—the will to life, the will to reconnect. The deceased cannot return, and that is accepted. But their legacies continue in the living, and at the funeral banquets, the after-meals, the sounds of conversation, laughter, and love entice sorrowing spirits to look, once again, toward ventures of the future, carrying with them the memories and wisdom of the past.

CHAPTER FIVE

Mourners' Rites
After the Funeral

Jacques Derrida wrote reflective and eloquent letters of condolence, memorial essays, eulogies, and funeral orations in response to the deaths of many of his well-known colleagues and contemporaries. His associates were thinkers and scholars of international stature: Roland Barthes, Paul De Man, Michel Foucault, Louis Althusser, Gilles Deleuze, Jean-François Lyotard, and others. They opened doors to the contemplation and understanding of language, mythologies, and ideological meanings for the twentieth century that continue to illuminate the very lives we live today. Derrida suggested that there are many solutions and responses to what has been called "following the death," or "on the occasion of the death," yet none really satisfactory in satisfying the debt we have to those who have lived before us and bequeathed to us so much in so many ways (Derrida 2001: 51). To remain loyal to the complex memories of beloved colleagues and family members, and to move forward in a life made better by the contributions made by those now gone, is a multifarious task. Contemplating how to carry the sadness but respect the complex meanings that these scholars freed for all of us to consider, Derrida reflected, "To keep alive, within oneself: is this the best sign of fidelity?" (Derrida 2001: 36).

Ongoing responses to the dead—for instance, the traditional Mexican American remembering and honoring of their deceased each year on the Day of the Dead and All Saints' Day, the Japanese

Americans' yearly celebration of Obon, and commemorative days of the Jews, Indo-Americans, and others—indicate that most human beings consciously strive to keep the memories of the departed alive "within oneself," as Derrida suggested. The "keeping alive" of those memories is maintained through myriad commemorative rituals and practices. For most people there seems to be a sense of responsibility in doing this. It is almost a matter of moral consciousness, or loyalty to the bond, in relation to the memory of deceased loved ones and friends. To honor them is to celebrate the lives they lived with respect and consideration. To clean the grave and offer food, or to light the candles and gaze on photographs of the deceased are focused efforts to remember their legacy and carry it into the future by way of memory. Over time, those memories are transmitted or transferred to the next generation and to new members of the family, and in that way the deceased continue to walk with the living.

Cemeteries in America, ongoing tributes to the dead, have traditionally been owned by municipalities, churches, or private fraternal or ethnic groups. In some rural areas, there are family cemeteries, and these grew up around remote industrial sites and in mining towns throughout the country as well. Individuals who lived far from established towns and villages had to take the process of funerary rituals and burial into their own hands. One old cemetery I visited high in American Fork Canyon in Utah held only twelve graves. I was told by my guide that they were the burial places of children who had died in a black diphtheria epidemic in the late 1800s. The families had to take care of their own. But contemporary Americans distance themselves from death, and for decades have turned over the process of decision making at the time of death to professionals who have established procedures (for specific fees) to take care of the needs of the public.

On the other hand, I believe that Americans are taking death and commemoration more seriously as we become an aging society. Earlier I mentioned the two, upright markers in the cemetery near Bowling Green State University. Around the base of both stones were many, many artifacts. It was late October, and in addition to pumpkins, candy, Mylar balloons, notes in ziplock bags, and a few books, were a high school letter jacket and a string of pearls. The event had occurred the prior year, and apparently friends were still suffering the loss and trying to maintain their memories and connections to these beloved peers.

Out of curiosity, I visited the stone carver who had made the matching grave markers and learned about the business of personal memorialization. There are memorialists and artisans who work together to help families personalize cemetery markers in great detail in order to represent the deceased as a unique individual to both family and other visitors to the cemetery. Jamie Walker, one of the memorialists in Toledo, Ohio, took me to a cemetery there where one woman had ordered a replication of an overstuffed chair, in granite and full-sized, as her grave monument because that was the place she had spent the last few years of her life. Her family saw that her wishes were carried through exactly as she had wished. Another grave site was marked with a large and stunning black, marbled stone with a bronze plaque attached. The young man buried there had died in a climbing accident, and his parents searched long to find exactly the right stone to mark his burial place. The plaque was a simple statement of his dates and name, and small, well-tended plants and groundcover surrounded the site.

In *Giving Voice to Sorrow: Personal Responses to Death and Mourning*, Steve Zeitlin and Ilana Harlow suggest that bereaved people find creative and personal ways to find a balance between remembrance and letting go. Though the separation through death of a loved one is never easy, they wrote, "Eventually, the emotional responses of sadness, horror, and anger over death make way for creative responses as people struggle to endure despite their grief" (Zeitlin and Harlow 2001: 20). Through creative responses to the memory of loved ones, the individualized cemetery markers described above provide comfort to the living—and even gentle humor, which must have been the intent of the woman who ordered the huge granite chair monument, which carries even the bumps and lumps of the chair's long use. I wondered, as I contemplated that "chair," how her family must feel when they visit there. It must evoke years of memories that help "keep alive" tender connectedness to her; yet I think it would make them smile, too.

In the Jewish tradition, the anniversary of a loved one's day of death is commemorated. The Askenazic Jews (deriving from central Europe) call the day *Yahrzeit,* while the Sephardic Jews (deriving from Spain) refer to it as *Annos* (literally "year time"). A light or candle is lit at sundown on the previous evening, and it is allowed to burn until the next sunset. The Kaddish is recited at services in the synagogue three times: in the evening, again at morning, and then again at afternoon services. *Yizkor* is a memorial service honoring the deceased, and it is recited at specified times during the year. "The Unveiling Ceremony," eleven months after the funeral, marks the end of the former mourning period for sons and daughters. It is the time of the formal dedication of the headstone, and if there are ten Jewish adults present, the Mourner's Kaddish may be recited.

A ritual behavior brought to the attention of millions by the popular and widely viewed film *Schindler's List* is worth noting. In the last part of the film, visitors to Schindler's burial place paid homage to him by leaving small stones there. This gesture is a symbol of respect and a visible sign that members of the family, or others, have come to visit, pay their respects, and remember the life of the deceased. In biblical times, graves were sometimes marked by a pile of stones. The tradition is ancient, and it provides a tangible response to memory. Anne Brener, in her book, *Mourning and Mitzvah,* suggests that the pebble on the gravestone may represent a marker to commemorate the visit, as well as a superstition "to weigh down spirits that they cease interfering in the lives of the living" (Brener 1993: 212).

As I visit cemeteries around the United States in my own scholarship and with tours sponsored by the American Cemetery and Gravestone Association, I have often noted the presence of pebbles and even palm-sized rocks placed on cemetery monuments marking the burials of people from various faiths. To me this represents a sharing of religious practice, again, a connectedness with one another by borrowing (or copying if that is more accurate) practices of others. That has always been a part of what Americans do. We borrow, syncretize, and make customs and practices of others fit our own needs. The pebbles and stones on Protestant and even Catholic markers probably mean many things to those who have placed them there, but, in the least of interpretations, they mark the honor of a visit to a remembered loved one.

Traditional Japanese Americans practice formal mourning and commemoration of the dead for seven weeks. Ceremonies held at the cemetery in remembrance of the deceased are held on the seventh, thirtieth, and one hundredth day following the death, but the forty-ninth day is generally accepted as the end of formal mourning. As mentioned in chapter 4, the mourning process has been relaxed somewhat, but older Japanese Americans still honor the age-old ritual customs. On the forty-ninth day after death, the spirit is said to leave for eternity. These ceremonies are often large gatherings, and a priest is sometimes present to instruct the deceased concerning progression through levels in the afterlife. These services are often followed by a generous dinner served in the family home or more often catered at a restaurant. In the home of the bereaved widow, widower, or parent, like the customs of Indo-Americans and Mexican Americans, a shrine is often set up and incense, rather than candles, is offered frequently. A small portion of food, particularly uncooked rice, is placed in a bowl near the shrine for the deceased when it is available. Unlike the Chinese who worship ancestors long dead, the Japanese and Japanese Americans honor their ancestors only as long as they are remembered by the living. Some families visit the grave site frequently and leave flowers, favorite foods, and beverages, but many wait for designated yearly events. Memorial services for the deceased are to be held one year after death, and again on commemoration of the second, third, seventh, thirteenth, seventeenth, twenty-third or twenty-fifth, twenty-seventh, and thirty-third year anniversaries. In Japan, the thirty-third anniversary of a death is usually the last commemorated, and sometimes a tree or plant is planted in honor of the deceased at that time. These traditions "are observed by descendants who probably did not know the deceased personally, but who feel an obligation to maintain proper filial relationships with the *kami* of their family" (Iwasaka and Toelken 1994: 25).

To honor the dead is a continuing national practice in the United States. Memorial Day, the last Monday in May as it is celebrated these days, is a national holiday. Neither religion nor ethnic heritage has much influence in the customs associated with Memorial Day. It is probably safe to say that most people don't think much about the reason Memorial Day was established and has become institutionalized. For most, it is a long weekend to enjoy the outdoors, go to sales at the mall, begin the camping season for the year, and be with the family. On the other hand, there are Americans who go to cemeteries to clean and decorate the graves of their deceased family and friends.

Memorial Day, once called Decoration Day, has been around since the end of the Civil War. There is a little discrepancy about the first practice of putting flowers on the graves of the Civil War dead. Though the first flowers may have been placed as early as 1864, in 1866, both in Columbus, Mississippi, and in Boalsburg, Pennsylvania, women decorated the graves. The controversy over where and exactly when the first official observance of this custom took place is less important than the homage itself. Both in the North and South, the soldiers were remembered and honored. The first formal Memorial Day observation was in May 1866, in Waterloo, New York, and President Lyndon Johnson recognized this town officially as the "birthplace" of Memorial Day. By 1873, it was "recognized as an official holiday, when New York State designated it as a legal holiday."[1] Government resolutions followed, and the Memorial Day celebrations, in honor of our military dead, continue to have been made official with the National Holiday Act, P.L. 90–363, in 1971. "Some Southern states adopted another Confederate Memorial Day holiday to honor just the Southern soldiers. This Confederate holiday is still celebrated in Texas on January 19, in Alabama, Florida, and Mississippi on April 26, in South Carolina on May 10, and in Louisiana and Tennessee on June 3" (Baskin-Jones 2004: 1).

Throughout the United States, families continue to clean and decorate the graves of their loved ones and the military dead. Settlers in early Utah, following traditions from the eastern United States where most of the early pioneers had been born, kept a special day of commemoration and celebration of the dead. Children were given tasks to mow the lawn and gather the grass clippings. The children also went to the foothills and along the ditch banks and gathered wildflowers of all kinds, including wild roses and buttercups. With these chores completed, families took the grass and flowers to the cemetery and scattered the grass clippings on the graves. The flowers were then laid on top of the grass. Flower containers were not used as they are today, and there was no lawn on the cemetery lots (Olsen, personal interview, July 29, 1997).

The tradition of cleaning and decorating the graves of loved ones (and strangers) on Memorial Day weekend continues to be a strong practice in many parts of the United States. Family members gather, go to the cemetery (or cemeteries) where their deceased loved ones are buried, and according to the regulations of the sexton, clean and decorate the graves. A family meal at home or in a park, usually of shared responsibility, either precedes or follows the trip to the cemetery.

Another commemorative custom giving evidence to survival of earlier traditions is to place lighted candles on the graves of loved ones on Christmas Eve, an old Scandinavian ritual. Folklorist Kristi Young described the family visit to her daughter's burial place on Christmas Eve, 2003:

> We had placed a red poinsettia and some painted Santa Claus figures we had made at home on the grave site earlier. That evening, we all went together. Laura's husband, Trevor, especially wanted to go, and her two-year-old, Will, went too. As we walked across the cemetery to Laura's burial place Christmas Eve, we could hear some families singing softly, and we noticed that some graves were marked by luminaries. Earlier in the day Jim [Kristi's husband] had placed some fresh flowers on the grave, but by evening, deer had already eaten part of them. It was a little windy, and we had three candles with ceramic bases we had planned to place by her gravestone. One of the girls went back to the car and got a pretty bag, and we set the lighted candles down into the bag so they would stay lit. We didn't stay very long, but it was a tender moment, and we all felt right about beginning that tradition for our family. (Young, personal interview, January 24, 2004)

In addition to these ethnic, religious, national, and family practices in relation to the ongoing commemoration of the dead, another aspect of American respect for the dead—in this case, paupers and the anonymous dead—is found in Hart Island, New York. A little-known burial ground in Long Island Sound, the cemetery has over one million graves, some dating back to the time of the Civil War. From stillborn babies of unwed mothers, to unidentified and unclaimed bodies of men and women, to the poverty stricken, the bodies are carefully fingerprinted, catalogued, and buried respectfully in plain pine coffins. The burial places are marked and numbered. Volunteers from a nearby correctional institution assist with the laborious task of digging orderly trenches and carefully placing the simple coffins in the proper order. Now and then, said Thomas McCarthy, director of historical services at Hart Island, a relative will claim a body, and take it to another burial place. This has to be accomplished within ten years after burial, but it does occur occasionally. Again, the dead are respected, and a service is performed for the living (McCarthy 2004, presentation).

Roadside Memorials

Roadside memorials have become commonplace throughout the United States, and these simple tributes appear in both rural and urban areas. They represent loved ones who have been killed in automobile accidents at that spot or later from injuries sustained there. Each one represents a tragic story, and the most poignant are those memorials that have more than one cross. Sometimes the memorials are only a simple white cross, and sometimes they are elaborately decorated with photographs, poems, prayers, red ribbons to signify death because of drunken driving, and plastic wreaths and/or flowers. The message from those who placed the memorials is both a homage to their dead and a warning to those who pass to drive carefully. These lovingly constructed memorials emerge from cultural practices deep in the history of Mexican Americans.

Descansos (resting places) is the name by which roadside memorials are known in the Hispanic culture. Long ago in Mexico and the American Southwest, even before the common use of horses or mules for pulling wagons, the tradition was for several men to shoulder a coffin after the funeral and carry it to the burial place. Often a long and arduous procession, it was necessary to rest along the way. The tradition was to mark the place where the participants rested with a branch, wildflowers, or even a simple cross made of two sticks fastened together with a leather cord. Eventually those resting places, or descansos, became regular stopping places for the long procession of the men, women, and children in attendance at the funeral and burial.

The coming of the automobile changed village life, and as Rudolfo Anaya wrote in *Descansos: An Interrupted Journey Tres Voces* (1995): "One word describes the change for me: violence. The *cuentos* [stories] of the people became filled with tales of car wrecks, someone burned by gasoline while cleaning a carburetor, someone crippled for life in an accident. The crosses along the country roads increased. Violent death had come with the new age. Yes, there was utility, the ease of transportation, but at a price. Pause and look at the cross on the side of the road, dear traveler, and remember the price we pay" (n.p.).

Looking at this phenomenon through the eyes of a scholar suggests that surviving humans need visible ways for expression of the grief that occurs at the sudden death of a beloved family member. These roadside memorials most often, but not always, represent deaths of the young, and the memorials have unstated, figurative signification: that is, the probable unheeded warnings of those who cared most for them, and the unwarranted guilt caregivers feel when their words are not accepted. Speeding by these memorials at 70 miles per hour really doesn't affect the outside observer emotionally, but they do serve as a reminder and warning to everyone to drive carefully.

Another popular memorialization increasingly in use today is the car window decal. An article in the *Washington Post* suggested that these decals may have been started with NASCAR culture. "Race cars have had numbers and sponsor decals for years. When two drivers died in the early 1990s, fans made black circles with the car numbers for their back windows. People put lettering on their race cars, 'In memory of . . .'"(Kinzie 2004: B01). In our identity-conscious United States, the decal signifies personal loss and tribute. After seeing his father buried at Arlington National Cemetery, André Lugo wanted to do more. "So one day Lugo, 21, came home and told his mother he wanted to show her something. On the back of his souped-up Ford Expedition, nearly the entire rear window was covered with a decal with silver script: 'In Loving Memory of C.S. M. Ret. Edward H. Lugo, February 16, 1951–March 15, 2004'" (Kinzie 2004: B01). Videos, tape-recorded funeral services, personalized caskets, Web sites, and other endeavors repeatedly reflect living America's regard for the deceased and the effort not to forget these valued ones who are absent from our midst.

Funerals and the customs surrounding them serve as a field lab for what is going on elsewhere in our society. Cross-cultural behaviors and the acceptance of change reflect a maturing American people. Not unlike the influence of music and literature in the United States, individualized memorializations can be translated into terms and ideas that define what most Americans now acknowledge as acceptable. The funerary rituals are a moment in time to mourn and to celebrate a life completed. We rally to the anguished bereaved, no matter the color, creed, or religion, and we have learned to transform our tragedies into shared anticipation of life to come. We connect, we build our webs of concern, and we persuade one another to move forward in comfort.

CHAPTER SIX

Explaining the Festival and the American Way of Death
Saying Good-bye

Americans are pragmatic people, and their views are sometimes so matter-of-fact as to be surprising to observers. I was told recently that in Chicago there is a boulevard with many funeral parlors along one side. Across from the mortuaries there are several restaurants with banquet halls that serve the post-funeral banquet needs. My acquaintance said that people talk about the restaurant they want for their own funeral banquet. She said that after a relative's funeral followed by a dinner at one of the nearby halls, her sister remarked that she was not impressed with the meal and felt it was an insult to their Aunt Jesse. She then expressed her desire to have her own funeral banquet at a specific restaurant nearby where the food would be much better.

In this, the potential deceased is looking to the enjoyment and comfort of those who will be present at her own funeral rituals. Without defining the funeral as a joyous expectation but still acknowledging the presence of family reunion and gaiety within that bounded time, Americans I have interviewed recognize that the final rite of passage reflects many of the same elements as the festival. Some bereaved, in fact, rejoice in their loved one's release from suffering and pain as my husband and his sisters did at their mother's passing after several years of struggle with a disabling and difficult cancer. Some are pragmatically accepting of death as a natural process of life, and some, many, are stunned and shocked by it yet are bolstered by supportive loved ones. In contemporary America, people simply do not think much about death ahead of time. With longer life spans assured by life-prolonging medical discoveries, better foods, and more concentration on preventative behaviors, death does not hover over life as it once did. Yet, the reality is, of course, that people still die everyday.

In *Time Out of Time*, Alessandro Falassi wrote "that festival commonly means a *periodically recurrent, social occasion in which, through a multiplicity of forms and a series of coordinated events, participate directly or indirectly to various degrees, all members of a whole community, united by ethnic, linguistic, religious,* [and] *historical bonds* [and sharing] *a world view*" (Falassi 1987: 2). The criteria for ritual mourning in all cultures fit this description; overall the explanation provides a framework that accurately describes most funerary behaviors. The death of a family member, friend, or other significant member of the human community calls for an acknowledgment of a life lived and completed. In all of the cultural and ethnic communities discussed in these chapters, death calls for a reversal of ordinary behavior. Daily social and occupational routines are disrupted, and people participate in a "series of coordinated events," united in a common worldview: These events are "sacred and profane, private and public, sanctioning tradition and introducing innovation, proposing nostalgic revivals, providing the expressive means for the survival of the most archaic folk customs, and celebrating the highly speculative and experimental avant-gardes of the elite fine arts" (Falassi 1987: 1). The rituals of death meet these same criteria.

If, as Falassi suggests, "the primary and most general function of the festival is to renounce and then to announce culture" (Falassi 1987: 3), then the funeral is also a festival celebration that renounces cultural death and announces, or affirms, a continuation of cultural life of the deceased in memory and perhaps literally. The associated foods and artifacts of the dead in the contemporary United States, from funeral potatoes to *Pan de Muerto* and from silk-lined caskets to marble columbaria, suggest that the generic human spirit wants to believe that life continues in some form. And, in the form of remembrance, it certainly does. Rituals at the time of death, that is, specific preparation of the body, funeral rites, food celebrations, and ongoing commemoration, construct memories. Those memories become symbols, and through family and friends and symbolic markings and letters on a cemetery stone, those memories live on indefinitely.

Symbolic characteristics and behaviors, Falassi further explained, must be present in ritual acts or rites. To further demonstrate the suggestion that funeral is festival, share an experiment in definition and substitute the word concept of "funeral" for "festival" in the following: "Such representation cannot be properly accomplished by reversal behavior or by rites of intensification alone, but only by the simultaneous presence in the name of festival [funeral] of all the basic behavioral modalities of daily social life . . . for instance from work, from play, from study, from religious observances. In sum, festival [funeral] presents a complete range of behavioral modalities, each one related to the modalities of normal daily life. At festival [funeral] times, people do something they normally do not; they abstain from something they normally do; they carry to the extreme behaviors that are usually regulated by measure; they invert patterns of daily social life" (Falassi 1987: 3). This demonstrates that funerary ritual, with all of its components and behavior modalities, follows the same pattern of the festival as Falassi defined it. Though it is a fractured time in the scheme of day-to-day living, the inverted patterns of daily social life are only temporary. These are important behaviors and evidence people's desire to hold onto the dead as long as possible through the phases of the traditions and until the putting away of the dead, the closure, occurs.

In the sometimes agonizing moments of the mourning process, permission is granted to mourn and privacy is respected. Privately or publicly, to cry, to suffer, to babble incoherently, and to release any of the myriad emotion that tumbles from deep within the psyche is sanctioned by nearly all of the cultures. Weeping and wailing has been so much a part of the funerary process, that in many cultures, for centuries past and even into the present, these were hired and paid behaviors to ensure their presence. Because of that angst, friends and family gather from far away, and grief is tenderly assuaged. The bereaved are supported, nurtured, and fed. Foods from the remembered past are proffered, physical reunions take place, and before long, laughter begins again. Life goes on, and the memories of these emotional but celebratory events continue to move forward with each participant.

Mary Douglas wrote that food is a form of identity that operates as a social communication. Food, deeply embedded with codes and messages, suggests "different degrees of hierarchy, inclusion and exclusion, boundaries and transactions across boundaries" (Douglas 1972: 61). Reflecting on some of the Navajo death taboos, for instance, not looking at the deceased any more than necessary to prepare the body for burial or not speaking the name of the deceased, which are coupled with deeply embedded codes and messages, helps to clarify a reification of boundaries with layered meanings to be respected by the Navajo, and also to be respected by the travelers who may observe and interact with them. The Navajo clans do not usually have an after-funeral feast. There may be a small, sustaining meal, but this is not a time for family gathering and celebration.

Falassi discusses ritual meanings of foods and celebratory banquets in terms of conspicuous consumption. There is often more food prepared than can be consumed, and the "traditional meals or blessed foods are one of the most frequent and typical features of the festival" representing "abundance, fertility, and prosperity" (Falassi 1987: 5):

> Ritual food is also a means to communicate with gods and ancestors, as in the Christian belief in the presence of Christ in the sacred meal of Communion, the Greek tradition that Zeus is invisibly present at the ritual banquets of the Olympic Games, or the practice of the Tsembanga Maring people of New Guinea, who raise, slaughter, and eat pigs for and with the ancestors. (Falassi: 1987: 5)

Another moment with an ancestor occurs when a Mexican American child places tortillas as the *ofrenda* (an offering made to the dead) at the home altar erected in honor of a departed loved one. In bountiful post-funeral meals, from Washington to Georgia, from Maine to New Mexico to Hawaii, communities of Americans of all derivations and skin colors take time out to reverse the grief and share whatever they can in "abundance, fertility, and prosperity."

Traditional foods require many hands to make them, and many mouths to eat them, and seldom is nutrition alone the main reason for their creation.

Folklorist Susan Kalčik echos the reality that "eating at such a time is a celebration of life in the face of death" (1997: 49). The preparation and consumption of specific foods occur at All Souls' Day in various countries around the world. "The English eat 'soul cakes'; the Italians eat a pastry called *fave dei morti* (beans of the dead); and the Mexicans eat *pan de muerto* (Bread of the Dead), as well as sweets in the shape of coffins, skeletons. . . . They are symbolically consuming death, thus celebrating the fact that they are living. But they are also symbolically expressing an acceptance of death and union with dead friends and family" (Kalčik 1997: 49).

As I researched, gathered, interviewed, and then wrote the text for this book, I realized once more how alike, and how different, the human family really is. There were hundreds of examples of almost identical behaviors in relation to honoring the deceased, and food was only one commonality. Coins, used metaphorically for good luck and safe journey to prepare the deceased for the ferryman's fee at the River Styx, appeared in Japanese, Taiwanese, Greek, and Italian traditions. The brass band appeared at both Chinese American funerals in San Francisco and the New Orleans Jazz Funerals in the deep South. Handkerchiefs given as a funeral memento appeared in European American society of early America, and again in the tradition of some contemporary Chinese Americans. Questioning by angels after death is a belief held by traditional Muslims, and an abstraction of the same is held as truth by the Mormons. The covering of mirrors appears in African American, Jewish, Hindu, and Chinese traditions. Neither Buddhists nor Navajos have formal funerary ceremonies for infants, and figuratively, like Christ, the Buddhist priests go bravely into Hell to teach and redeem the spirits there. So alike, and yet so different.

There is an attempt to create original ceremonies to honor the deceased, but the replication of the ceremonies throughout the country suggests that there are boundaries to appropriate memorialization. Releasing butterflies or doves has become almost popular, and my husband and I attended a funeral viewing recently that had a decidedly Western motif with saddles, ten-gallon hats, ropes, and other corral equipment displayed on sawhorses around the viewing area.

The Cremation Association of America was founded in Detroit, Michigan, in 1913, and by 1919, there were approximately seventy crematories in the United States. Most were operated within the confines of the cemetery. *Purified by Fire: A History of Cremation in America* (2001) by Stephen Prothero tells the fuller history of the practice of cremation in the United States. Cremation has become an accepted form of "burial," but even with that finality of the physical body, there are distinct variations in the styles with which the cremains are treated. Cremation is more common than burial in some states, including Hawaii, Nevada, Washington, Alaska, Oregon, Montana, and Arizona. It is the preferred method among the upper socioeconomic strata of American society. There are religious groups that seem to prefer cremation over traditional burial: Christian Scientists, Unitarians, Episcopalians, Buddhists, and Hindus, and its use is also common among AIDS victims. The Roman Catholic Church lifted its ban on cremations in 1963, and Catholic cremations have kept pace with the rest of the U.S. population since then. There is little difference in the ratio of men to women in choosing cremation, and, statically the "ratio of cremations to deaths reached 25 percent nationwide in 1999, when 1,366 crematories incinerated well over half a million bodies in the United States" (Prothero 2001: 189).

There have been many articles, chapters, and books written about what happens to the body after death and about the American funeral industry and its response to the bereaved. There are professional memorialists who serve almost as counselors to the bereaved in assisting them to design appropriate tributes to the dead. Custom-designed Web sites, cemetery stones, or personalized columbaria are created to sensitively honor and enshrine the personality of the deceased. Much of the American public has become somewhat more informed about the costs of burial and memorialization, and there are points of accountability for the funeral industry itself regarding expenses. Most mortuary staff and memorialists offer a wide range of products and services to meet the budget restraints of the surviving family members.

There is, of course, endless speculation about whether or not the spirit or soul of the deceased individual survives the death of the body.[1] Most belief systems, both ancient and more recent ones, suggest that there is, somehow, a continuation of the essence of the deceased's personality. Many believe that the continuation is literally the memories held by the living of the dead. Others believe that there are little-understood dimensions where the spirits of the dead reside, categorized by the consequence of their choices and behavior in mortality. Some Christian belief systems believe in progression and improvement of the spirit, even in death, and others believe that when the last breath is drawn, the fate of the individual is sealed.

The Muslim belief is that the spirit literally survives death and communicates with the living. Through dreams and other appearances, it is believed that the dead can communicate both directions and their wishes to the living. On the other hand, the living are believed to be able to petition the dead for favors both in this world and in the next. The belief is that communication can go both ways.

Mormons, or LDS, are also literal believers in an active and cognizant afterlife. Both in the past centuries and this one, it has not been an unusual practice for a verbal message to be given to a dying person to relate to a spirit "on the other side." Throughout human history, there has been a desire to believe that life continues in some familiar form or another, as evidenced by ancient burial practices such as placing artifacts and foods in the burial place in case they may be needed in the afterlife. Even today great assortments of items are placed in the caskets of loved ones. From some points of view, to see the deceased actively participating in a video or on an individualized Web site is assurance enough of the permanent continuation of a form of life.

As I researched material for this text, I came to the realization that *dignity* in regard to death is the most important component. There is really no substitute for that concept, and it was present in every group discussed here. The sweet, nearly festive activities that surround the dying and bereaved in these varied but representative cultures suggest that cultural plurality in the United States is alive and well, and that respect for the unique differences of one another has become almost a given rather than a divisive element in our society. Dawn Han, an American lawyer born in Tawain said: "I believe the ceremonies that mark the closure of one's life on earth reflect immensely the cultures that breed them" (Han, personal correspondence, January 13, 2003). The acceptance of the inevitable includes dignity and comforting rituals, traditional, invented, and syncretic, that serve the people of America well. In this country, we enjoy the valuable luxury of toleration and free choice in making decisions regarding the farewells to our dead.

The late Elizabeth Kübler-Ross wrote that "those who have the strength and love to sit with a dying patient in the *silence that goes beyond words* will know that this moment is neither frightening nor painful, but a peaceful cessation of the functioning of the body. Watching a peaceful death of a human being reminds us of a falling star; one of a million lights in a vast sky that flares up for a brief moment only to disappear into the endless night forever" (Kübler-Ross 1997: 276). Each one of us is a part of the vastness of humanity, and each person who lives on the earth for any period of time is somehow connected to other lives. No matter how brief one's light may have been, life is a precious experience, and we are all influenced by one another's existence.

Epilogue
Looking Forward

It takes time to let go of a loved one. Some individuals firmly believe that bodies will be resurrected through the power of God; some people believe that bodies will be revived through the power of science. Some believe that the physical body will somehow be absorbed into a greater, universal whole; others believe that as long as people retain memory of living individuals, the metaphorical spirit of the departed individual lives. There is a folk belief that living memory of an individual lasts for about one hundred years. That is, at most, the longest time those living at the time of the death will live. Fame, of course, can guarantee eternal remembrance, and that may be for better and for worse. In many families, sharing a favorite food of the deceased, telling anecdotes, or using a favorite scent or favorite flower of a dead loved one can bring back warm memories. Regardless, it is difficult to "let go" of a beloved family member, friend, or even well-known public figure who has served humanity well. Gary Laderman, author of *Rest in Peace* (2003), stated well our collective need to part gently: "Most Americans do not want the dead body to disappear too quickly. But on the other hand, they do not want it lingering around for too long. A brief intimate moment with the dead—looking at the face, touching the casket, being in the presence of the corpse for a short time—is an ingrained ritual gesture that brings meaningful, and material, order out of the chaos of death" (Laderman 2003: 211).

A company named Alcor provides a service to the deceased called cryonic preservation. In cryonics, the body is frozen, and a several-hours-long Alcor laboratory procedure carefully infuses it with a chemical solution that prevents potentially damaging ice formation in the tissues. The theory is that at some later time, molecular activity can be revived in the deceased, and because of advanced medical research, the death will be reversed resulting in revival of the apparently deceased body. The process is called vitrification (deep cooling and solidification without freezing), and after the laboratory preparation, the bodies are eventually placed in aluminum containers immersed in liquid nitrogen at a temperature of −196 degrees Celsius for long-term maintenance.

The Alcor Web site (http://www.alcor.org) informs us that the company was founded more than thirty years ago (1972) and is currently endowed with more than two million dollars donated by wealthy Alcor members. The goal of the company is reversible suspended animation, and the current membership of the organization is now around one thousand. Though Alcor complies with state laws concerning "the transport and disposition of human remains," it is not "explicitly recognized in the laws of any state in the United States." There is some hostility to the practice both from scientists and regulatory officials, but, as the Web site states: "Despite these uncertainties, the United States enjoys a strong cultural tradition to honor the wishes of terminal patients. We believe that the freedom to choose cryonics is constitutionally protected, and so far courts have agreed. We are hopeful that we will be able to continue performing cryonics without technical compromise, under state supervision where necessary, for the indefinite future." The cryonics Web page suggests that "the spiritual status of cryonics patients is the same as frozen human embryos, or unconscious medical patients. When properly examined, cryonics has been endorsed by both clergy and theologians." The practice is sustained by the belief that future medicine will include mature nanotechnology, and that through molecular healing, these preserved bodies will be revived. At this point, the site states, there are about one hundred bodies preserved by this method, and "more than one thousand people have made legal and financial arrangements for cryonics with one of several organizations, usually by means of affordable life insurance." Cryonics is an attempt at a scientifically controlled resurrection, years, perhaps hundreds of years, into the future. For those who can afford it, it is a scientific experiment in hope.

As noted earlier, cremation is rising in popularity in the United States as a way of disposing of human remains. The origin of the United States's cremation movement is difficult to define, but an article published by Sir Henry Thompson called "Cremation: The Treatment of the Body after Death" in the January 1874 *Contemporary Review* is the probable catalyst for the rising presence of cremation among Euro-American citizens. Cremation is less expensive than buying a cemetery plot and monument. It is clean and professionally administered, and because of concerns about land use and ecological issues, it is an environmentally friendly option for handling human remains. Some Native American tribes had been practicing cremation on these shores for undefined centuries, but the European Americans struggled for generations with the concept as not being genteel.

In crematoriums throughout the United States, baby boomers and Asian Americans have led the way in a national culture that seems to remain both in the mood for self-styled rituals, and, at the same time, trends toward a more traditional relationship between the clergy and church membership. A ritual indicates a transformation, mutation, or at least a change of some kind. Rituals are separate from ordinary, daily life, and are performed with the concept of remembrance. To celebrate an individual life is a tradition at both birth and death in most cultures, and the concept of cremation, though ancient, carries both old and new significations for today's bereaved.

An Indo-American son may spend time with other living family members bidding farewell to a loved one, and then by ancient custom and tradition, he is to light the crematory flame, or, as Prothero wrote, hit "the start button" (Prothero 2001: 204). In my husband's Protestant family, his beloved aunt arranged for a traditional funerary celebration of her life, and then arranged for her body to be whisked away and cremated after the family had adjourned from the mortuary. Her remains were to be buried at her grave site and marked with an ordinary, engraved tombstone. In the Forest Lawn Cemetery, in Buffalo, New York, cremains (ashes) can be interred in small metal urns and placed in earthen berms, or mounds of earth, with tasteful plantings of flowering blossoms and evergreens adorning the burial place. Scattering cremains is also an option, and in the last half century, cremated remains have been scattered in places as unrelated as the ocean to Disney World. Disney World banned scattering on their property, as have other locations, but the practice continues, and there are several businesses that will assist the friends or families in the process for a modest fee.

Natural memorial parks, or green burials, are another option that people can consider either for their own bodies or for those of their loved ones. For thousands of years, humans have buried the deceased simply and efficiently in deserts and forests or wherever they found themselves. Natural memorial park concept requires that the deceased be either cremated or, if not, that the body has not been embalmed. There are to be no unusual chemical substances to leak into the ecosystem. If a casket is used, it is to be of a natural, biodegradable material. Not unlike the practices of some Native Americans, the burial is simple and natural in a privately owned, parklike setting that will remain in its natural garden state. In my interview with Barre Toelken, I was told that sometimes Navajos will simply take the body, after preparation for burial, to a place on the reservation and bury it without ceremony (Toelken, personal interview, December 30, 2002). In some Native American cultures, if there is an undertaker nearby to take care of the body and burial, the process may be gratefully turned over to the professionals because of the traditional fear of provoking anger in the ghosts of the dead. The method varies with the circumstances.

In the typical Protestant culture, the deceased spends time arrayed in his or her best for a viewing, within banks of flowers, at a funeral home before burial. In the Chinese American and Japanese American cultures, the presence of Buddhist priests provide comfort for the living and honor to the dead, and the casket and wreaths hold special significations indicating respect and honor. In these three cultures, the deceased are sometimes buried, sometimes cremated. These are typical and traditional practices accepted by most belief systems

across the nation. On the other hand, California's Thresholds Family
Directed Funerals assists families in creating their own ceremony and
rituals. This funerary business suggests that "some of the rituals families find very healing are: bathing and purifying the body; dressing the
body; creating altars and sacred space; and using art as a means to ex-
press and work through their love and loss" (http://www.thresholds.
us/index.asp). Their philosophy is that better healing can take place
if the families can literally work through the grieving process by participating in the details of caring for the body.

Another style of burial, prohibitive to most because of costs, is the
space burial. For some 150 people, as of 2003, arrangements have been
made for their cremains to be sent out into space. Space burial, that is
using a rocket to launch the cremated ashes into orbit, is an expensive
procedure. Because of the difficulty and costliness, only a small amount
of ashes (1g to 7g), those which can be contained in a lipstick-sized tube,
are actually deployed. A Web site (http://www.brainyencyclopedia.com/
encyclopedia/s/sp/space_burial.html) suggests that any remaining cremains may be buried at sea or in the earth.

The first space burial, *Earthview 01: Founders Flight*, was
launched April 21, 1997, and carried samples of the remains of twenty-
four people to an altitude of 11 km (38,000 miles) above the Canary
Islands. Partial cremains of famous people buried on this flight were
Gene Roddenberry (1921–1991, creator of *Star Trek*) and Timothy
Leary (1920–1996, American writer, psychologist, and drug cam-
paigner). The second launch of cremains included those of Dr. Eu-
gene Shoemaker (1928–1997, astronomer who discovered the comet
Shoemaker-Levy 9). A sample of his cremains were launched January 7, 1998, within the Lunar Prospector probe and reportedly "im-
pacted the moon near the lunar south pole on 4:42 A.M. Central
Daylight Time, on July 31, 1999" (http://www.brainyencyclopedia.
com/enclyclopedia/s/sp/space_burial.html). According to this same
Web site, only one company, Celestis, currently offers space burials.
In time that may change as the cost and difficulties of the process di-
minish and other companies enter the market.

From auto decal memorials to memorial collages and collections
displayed at mortuaries in honor of the deceased, Americans contin-

ue to invent new and meaningful tributes to our dead. *The Houston Chronicle* printed an article called "New in funerals: wrapped caskets," which described White Light, a company in Dallas, Texas, which has invented a shrink-wrap process for caskets. Decorated with appealing scenes, the covering provides "the first practical means to truly personalize a casket. . . . We have hundreds of scenes available, everything from a golf course to the Last Supper" (Hoffman 1998). The White Light company will fill custom orders for shrink-wrap casket decorations that range from religious symbols, to personal or famous personage photographs, to mountains, ski slopes, or whatever else may be desired. Called the "Epilogue" shrink-wrap, the cost ranges between $2,500 and $3,000. It is not yet available at all funeral homes, because it is relatively new and unique. Undoubtedly, though, there will be consumers who will desire to honor their loved ones in this way.

Another variant on permanent placement of cremains recently came over one of my Internet sites. A company named Eternal Reefs (http://www.eternalreefs.com) has combined "a cremation urn, ash scattering, and a burial at sea into one meaningful permanent environmental tribute to life," as it explains in its advertising. Suggesting that many people keep traditional cremation urns for decades, not quite able to do a scattering, the Eternal Reef, that is, a cremation urn secured in an ocean reef, may "provide the closure for the family that they seek and need." For those who love the ocean, and they are many of course, that may be a reasonable and comforting memorial.

Cybermemorials, that is, Web sites that picture the dead, have grown in popularity and can include color photographs, sounds, and even motion pictures. These sites feature permanent images as well as music and guest books. Because they are on the World Wide Web, they can be accessed from any location and are particularly useful to friends and family who may not have been able to attend the local services for the deceased. Links to chat rooms can be arranged also so that people who are mourning the loss of a loved one can celebrate the life in communication with one another. There are virtual cemeteries where flower icons and even online memorial services can be arranged, and many of the sites also provide memorials for pets.[1]

From Web sites to shrink-wrap, honoring the dead in the ways perceived to be most appropriate by personal arrangement, family, friends, or loved ones continues. The burial places, scattering sites, and ceremonial locale will be visited frequently or infrequently by the living for as long as the memory of the deceased survives. Either through the guidance of clergy or other religious leaders, or by the creativity of our own families and friends, we both mourn and celebrate our dead. We acknowledge them by maintaining their lives in our own memories. Ancient religious symbols such as the willow (which represents mourning for the loss of earthly life), the hourglass (the swift passage of time), the circle (perfection, eternity), the lily (purity and virtue), the Star of David (Jewish symbol of divine protection throughout eternity), representations of the family of Christ and other meaningful contemporary secular symbols (toys, golf bags, motorcycles, square dancers, menorah, crosses, sea gulls, Asian calligraphy, eagles) continue to mark the headstones and urns of today. In formal garden cemeteries across the nation, in green space, and in the atmosphere around our world, we are accompanied in life by those who have lived before.

In enormously popular books like *Life After Life* (thirty-five printings through 1981), to various religious scriptures, to the popularity of books on contemporary death and dying, Americans continue to seek a peek beyond the veil of mortality. We send our beloved dead off with the hope of seeing them again somewhere, someplace. Even in late age and poor health, we Americans attempt to enjoy life, we enjoy each other, we love to celebrate and laugh, and death is not a welcome guest in our community. But the reality is that it is among us, and it is a part of the natural cycle of life. What we are able to learn about death as we move along through life, Raymond Moody reminded us, "may make an important difference in the way we live our lives" (Moody 1981: 84).

Victor Turner closed his book, *The Ritual Process,* with a final comment about society being a process rather than a thing, "a dialectical process with successive phases of structure and communitas" (Turner 1969: 203). He wrote that there is a human "need" to participate in ritual and symbol, and that the superior quest is for "symbolic communitas" (Turner 1969: 203). So, in our journey, we awaken at some point to the reality that our behavior has consequences and that we need one another. We begin to understand that, like a creature emerging from a cocoon, we have freedom, and with that freedom comes social and cultural responsibility. We transform, and we connect to a greater world of beauty with our like creatures. Our joy of life comes through the complex webs we weave over time, and at the end of our weaving, we will be remembered for who we are and what our lives have meant to those with whom we have linked.

Notes

Prologue

1. This concept of custom and tradition is taken from Eric Hobsbawm and Terence Ranger, eds., *The Invention of Tradition* (1983/1997: 3). "The decline of 'custom' inevitably changes the tradition with which it is habitually intertwined."

2. In *Folkloristics: An Introduction*, Robert A. Georges and Michael Owen Jones defined the term folkloristics as *"folklore studies* or *folklife research"*; they also defined it as an area of academic pursuit that "denotes the study of folklore as a discipline with its own assumptions, concepts, lexicon, issues, and hypotheses" (Georges and Jones 1995: 1, 23).

3. In *Rabelais and His World*, Mikhail Bakhtin wrote that "No meal can be sad. Sadness and food are incompatible. . . . The banquet always celebrates a victory and this is part of its very nature" (Bakhtin 1984: 283).

4. Marshall McLuhan, *Understanding Media: The Extensions of Man* (New York: Signet Books, 1964).

5. It is difficult, according to Victor Turner in *The Ritual Process*, "to find the appropriate relationship between structure and communitas under the *given* circumstances of time and place, to accept each modality when it is paramount without rejecting the other, and not to cling to one when its present impetus is spent" (Turner 1969: 139). Death of a cared for relative, friend, or sometimes an unknown loved one of someone we know and respect, brings with it a forced, inescapable adjustment to change. Appropriate response, colored by emotion, demands time and positive support from a community of people to assist the bereaved in their appropriate adjustment.

6. In *Of Corpse: Death and Humor in Folklore and Popular Culture*, Peter Narváez wrote that the "Paradoxical juxtapositions of death and humor in today's world are on the rise, and an understanding of traditional

combinations of this nature may assist us in coping with present realities" (Turner 2003: 5).

7. In Jan Brunvand's *American Folklore: An Encyclopedia*, Angus Kress Gillespie wrote that festival is "a time set aside for celebration. . . . At the most basic level, there are homegrown, grass-roots festivals organized by and for a particular community" (Brunvald 1996: 249). The funerary festival or celebration represents a time of celebration in honor of a life lived and completed, and this has been the practice of groups in the United States for centuries.

8. Arnold van Gennep wrote the classic text *The Rites of Passage* (Chicago: Viking Press, 1960). In it, he stated that "On first considering funeral ceremonies, one expects rites of separation to be their most prominent component, in contrast to rites of transition and rites of incorporation which should be only slightly elaborated. A study of the data, however, reveals that rites of separation are few in number and very simple, while the transition rites have a duration and complexity sometimes so great, that they must be granted a sort of autonomy. Furthermore, those funeral rites which incorporate the deceased into the world of the dead are most extensively elaborated and assigned the greatest importance" (Gennep 1960: 146). While this is true of some traditional and fundamental belief systems, I maintain that most of contemporary American funerary ritual is created and performed for the comfort and edification of the living.

9. Gary Laderman's books, *The Sacred Remains: American Attitudes toward Death, 1799–1883* (1996) and *Rest in Peace: A Cultural History of Death and the Funeral Business in Twentieth-Century America* (2003), are the first full-scale studies of American funeral industry development. Both books are positive in tone, and they remind the reading public of the vital role the funeral industry plays in modern society.

10. According to an essay in *The Journal of American Culture* (2003) by Samuel Chambers: "The realm of the specter is a place in which characters renegotiate boundaries, a place where they can try to articulate [to] their ghosts (that is to themselves) the very terms of their identity" (Chambers 2003: 29). American identity is often associated with food, and the settings of *Six Feet Under* often reflect that nurturing association as a response to tension and conflicted emotion.

One. Funerals as Festivals

1. More Reagan facts can be found on the Web site http://www.reagan.utexas.edu/resource/handout/Rrfacts.htm.

Two. The Final Passage

1. When a Latter-day Saint male reaches the age of nineteen, he is usually expected to serve a two-year mission for the church. It is at that time

that most young men visit the temple to receive instructions about the meaning of mortality and make their life vows and commitments to God. Young women, if they choose, may serve an eighteen-month mission when they are twenty-one, and it is usually at that time that they visit the temple for the first time. Though many Latter-day Saint couples are married in the temple, many are not and often go to the temple to receive their instructions (endowments) later in life. After dedication, the temples of The Church of Jesus Christ of Latter-day Saints are not open to the public, but prior to dedication, they are often open to the public for tours. The intent is not to create a secret or mysterious ambiance about the temple and the ceremonies that take place there, but rather to respect the sacred nature of vows and covenants made there with solemn piety.

Three. Wakes and Other Amusements

1. Richard Meyer commented about books similar to Bergin's, saying, "The chief culprits . . . are a number of small and cheaply made booklets—sometimes in the shape of gravestones—with grotesque titles such as *The Itty-Bitty Bathroom Book of Bodacious Tombstone Epitaphs* (okay, that's a bit of an exaggeration, but close enough to make the point)" (Meyer 2003: 142). Bergin's book, *The Definitive Guide to Underground Humor*, doesn't quite fit Meyer's description, but the stories included are not clearly documented. They are fun, but perhaps carry the anonymous character of urban lore.

Four. Funeral Biscuits and Funeral Feasts

1. Charles Camp wrote that responses from neighbors and friends cross cultural barriers, and that comforting extension of kindness to the bereaved family is often conveyed in the form of a casserole. "In is interesting to note," Camp wrote, "that unlike person-to-person gifts, food given at the time of a neighbor's death is given household-to-household, and generally eschews the types of food ordinarily given—cakes, pies, and cookies, which perhaps convey cheerier sentiments than the occasion calls for. More common are bread, meat, cheese, salads, and other foods that need little preparation for a meal, and may be set out for family and guests as the need arises" (1989: 103).

2. William Weaver, in his text *American Eats: Forms of Edible Folk Art*, wrote: "The funeral biscuit . . . was one means of cementing [the] connection between community and its landscape. These biscuits, saved from one funeral to the next, served as reminders of particular individuals, just as rows of headstones in the churchyard, decorated with similar motifs, reminded all who passed the 'story' of each person buried there" (Weaver 1989: 5).

3. Gary Laderman, quoting a source from 1856 (Sargeant) wrote that "Every one, as he entered, took off his hat, with his left hand, smoothed

down his hair, with his right, walked up to the coffin, gazed upon the corpse, made a crooked face, passed on to the table, took a glass of his favorite liquor, went forth upon the plat, before the house, and talked politics, or of the new road, or compared crops, or swapped heifers or houses, until it was time to lift" (Weaver 1996: 32).

4. In *The Theory of the Leisure Class* (1899), Thorstein Veblen, an economist and social commentator, debunked many of the practices of the nineteenth century including the debilitating women's dress (restrictive corsets and laces) of the Victorian Age, academic pomp and circumstance, and other, seemingly entrenched, rather useless (as far as Veblen could observe) cultural constructions and behaviors.

5. Toelken also noted that many Navajos have fruit trees, and they will eat assorted vegetables when they can get them. Locally produced corn, beans, squash, and even tobacco are usually present at Navajo gatherings. He also said that the Navajos have adapted many Mexican foods for common use. The Navajo taco, a popular food, is made by piling beans, lettuce, and chili on top of a piece of fry bread (Toelken, December 30, 2002).

Five. Mourners' Rites

1. Memorial Day information is available online at http://www.army. mil/cmh-pg/faq/memday/MD-Dev.htm.

Six. Explaining the Festival and the American Way of Death

1. The funeral or memorial service, in some minds, somehow changes the status of the deceased soul in the perspective of those providing the ceremony. It seems to end the mourners' anxiety for the departed individual, and the ritual helps to solemnly release the deceased into the society of the departed. The after-funeral dinner then provides a period for the bereaved to be nurtured into returning to interaction and connectedness with close family and friends.

Epilogue

1. A Web site that provides online memorial services, as well as flower icons to decorate those sites, is http://www.memorialonthenet.com/

References

Achaya, K.T. *Indian Food: A Historical Companion.* Delhi: Oxford University Press, 1994.

Allen, Woody. Food Reference Web site. <http://www.foodreference.com/html/qfunerals.html>. Accessed June 20, 2005.

Amish. <http://www.chaplaincare.navy.mil/Amish.htm>. Accessed June 16, 2005.

Anaya, Rudolfo. *Descansos: An Interrupted Journey Tres Voces.* No city: El Norte, 1995.

Bakhtin, Mikhail. *Rabelais and His World.* Bloomington, Ind.: Indiana University Press, 1984.

Barthes, Roland. *Mythologies.* New York: The Noonday Press, 1990.

Baskin-Jones, Michelle. "Why Do We Celebrate Memorial Day?" <http://dying.about.com/od/faqsquickfacts/aMemorial_Day.htm>. 2004. Accessed July 14, 2004.

Bergin, Edward. *The Definitive Guide to Underground Humor.* Waterbury, Connecticut: Offbeat Publishing, 1996.

Brandes, Stanley. "Calaveras: Literary Humor in Mexico's Day of the Dead." In *Of Corpse: Death and Humor in Folklore and Popular Culture*, ed. Peter Narváez. Logan: Utah State University Press, 2003.

———. "The Day of the Dead, Halloween, and the Quest for Mexican National Identity." *Journal of American Folklore* Vol. 111, no. 442 (Fall 1998): 359–80.

Brener, Anne. *Mourning and Mitzvah: A Guided Journal for Walking the Mourner's Path through Grief to Healing.* Woodstock, Vt.: Jewish Lights Publishing, 1993.

Brewer, J. Mason. *American Negro Folklore.* New York: Quadrangle, The New York Times Book Company, 1968.

Brodkin, Karen. *How Jews Became White Folks & What That Says about Race in America.* New Brunswick, N.J.: Rutgers University Press, 2000.

Bronner, Simon J. *Following Tradition.* Logan: Utah State University Press, 1998.

Brunvand, Jan Harold, ed. *American Folklore: An Encyclopedia.* New York & London: Garland Publishing, Inc., 1996.

———. *The Study of American Folklore.* 4th edition. New York: W.W. Norton Company, Inc., 1998.

Buerkle, Jack V., and Danny Barker. *Bourbon Street Black: The New Orleans Black Jazzman.* London, Oxford, New York: Oxford University Press, 1973.

Camp, Charles. *American Foodways: What, When, Why and How We Eat in America.* Little Rock, Ark.: August House, Inc., 1989.

Cantwell, Robert. *Ethnomimesis: Folklife and the Representation of Culture.* Chapel Hill & London: The University of North Carolina Press, 1993.

Caputo, John D. *The Prayers and Tears of Jacques Derrida: Religion without Religion.* Bloomington, Ind.: Indiana University Press, 1997.

Carmichael, Elisabeth, and Chloë Sayer. *The Skeleton at the Feast: The Day of Dead in Mexico.* Austin: University of Texas Press, 1992.

Carrell, Amy. "Humor Communities." *Humor* 10: 11–24. 1997.

Chambers, Samuel E. "Telepistemology of the Closet: or, The Queer Politics of *Six Feet Under*." *The Journal of American Culture* Vol. 26, no. 1 (March 2003): 24–41.

Child Trends Data Bank. <http://www.childtrendsdatabank.org>. Accessed June 20, 2005.

Chu, Lenora. "Buddhist Burial Practices and the U.S. 'Post-Life' Industry. *Asian Week Archives.* June 12–21, 2000. <http://www.asianweek. com/2000_06_15biz2_trendtrack.html>. Acccessed August 4, 2004.

Colman, Penny. *Corpses, Coffins, and Crypts: A History of Burial.* New York: Henry Holt and Company, 1997.

Coward, Harold, ed. *Life after Death in World Religions.* Maryknoll, N. Y.: Orbis Books, 1997.

Cragg, Kenneth. *The Dome and the Rock: Jerusalem Studies in Islam.* London: S.P.C.K., 1964.

Daybell, Chad. *One Foot in the Grave: The Strange But True Adventures of a Cemetery Sexton.* Springville, Utah: Bonneville Books, 2001.

Deetz, James, and Edwin S. Dethlefsen. "Death's Head, Cherub, Urn, and Willow." In *Material Culture Studies in America: An Anthology,* Thomas J. Schlereth, ed. Nashville, Tenn.: The American Association for State and Local History, 1989.

Denny, Frederick M. *Islam and the Muslim Community*. San Francisco: Harper and Row Publishers, 1987.

Derrida, Jacques. *The Work of Mourning*. Chicago and London: The University of Chicago Press, 2001.

———. *The Gift of Death*. Chicago and London: The University of Chicago Press, 1995.

Douglas, Mary. "Deciphering a Meal." *Daedalus* 101 (Winter 1972): 54–72.

Dresser, Norine. *Multicultural Celebrations: Today's Rules of Etiquette for Life's Special Occasions*. New York: Three Rivers Press, 1999.

Duyff, Roberta Larson. *Food Folklore: Tales and Truths about What We Eat*. Minneapolis, Minn.: Chronimed Publishing (The American Dietetic Association), 1999.

Edgette, J. Joseph. "The Epitaph and Personality Revelation." *Cemeteries and Gravemarkers: Voices of American Culture*. Logan: Utah State University Press, 1989.

Ellis, Bill. *Raising the Devil: Satanism, New Religions, and the Media*. Lexington: The University Press of Kentucky, 2000.

Eternal Reefs. <http://www.eternalreefs.com>. Accessed June 22, 2005.

Falassi, Alessandro, ed. *Time Out of Time: Essays on the Festival*. Albuquerque: University of New Mexico Press, 1987.

Fine, Gary Alan. "Humour and Communication Discussion." In *It's a Funny Thing*, ed. Anthony J. Chapman and Hugh J. Foot, New York: Pergamon Press, 1997a.

———. "Humor in Situ: The Role of Humor in Small Group Culture." In *It's a Funny Thing*, ed. Anthony J. Chapman and Hugh J. Foot, New York: Pergamon Press, 1997b.

"Fly Away: The Great Migration." <http://www.northbysouth.org/1999/flyaway.htm>. Accessed April 4, 2003.

Fox, Sarah Alisabeth. "'There Was a Beautiful Formation, And Then the Cloud Went Right Over My Head': A Folkloric Analysis of the Downwinder Tale." Unpublished paper. Utah Folklore Society Conference. Salt Lake City, Utah, February 12, 2005.

Freud, Sigmund. *Jokes and Their Relation to the Unconscious*. Trans and ed. James Strachey. New York: W.W. Norton, 1960 (1905).

Fussell, Betty. *I Hear America Cooking: A Journey of Discovery from Alaska to Florida—The Cooks, the Recipes, and the Unique Flavors of Our National Cuisine*. New York: Viking Penguin Inc., 1986.

Gallagher, Carol. *American Ground Zero: The Secret Nuclear War*. Cambridge, Mass.: MIT Press, 1993.

Gambino, J. *Blood of My Blood*. New York: Doubleday & Company, 1975.

Gennep, Arnold van. *The Rites of Passage*. Chicago: The University of Chicago Press (Phoenix Books), 1960.

Georges, Robert A., and Michael Owen Jones. *Folkloristics: An Introduction*. Bloomington and Indianapolis: Indiana University Press, 1995.

Grant, William H. Personal Interview. June 22, 2003. Provo, Utah.

Hafferty, Frederick W. "Cadaver Stories and the Emotional Socialization of Medical Students." *Journal of Health and Social Behavior* Vol. 29 (December 1988): 344–56.

Han, Dawn. Personal Correspondence to Author. January 13 and 17, 2003.

Harlow, Ilana. "Creating Situations: Practical Jokes and the Revival of the Dead in Irish Tradition." *Journal of American Folklore* Vol. 110, no. 436 (Spring 1997): 140–68.

Hawthorne, Nathaniel. *The Scarlet Letter*. New York: Signet Classic/Penguin Group, 1980.

Height, Dorothy I., and The National Council of Negro Women, Inc. *The Black Family Dinner Quilt Cookbook: Health Conscious Recipes and Food Memories*. New York: A Fireside Book/Simon and Schuster, 1994.

Herzog, Karen. "Mourning Dishes: Funeral Meals Go beyond Nourishment for Family and Friends." *Milwaukee Journal Sentinel: JS Online*. June 11, 2002. <http://www.jsonline.com/entree/cooking/June02/50286.asp>

Hobsbawm, Eric, and Terence Ranger. *The Invention of Tradition*. New York: Press Syndicate of the University of Cambridge, 1997.

Hoffman, Ken. "New in Funerals: Wrapped Caskets." *Houston Chronicle*. June 30, 1998, p. 1.

Holloway, Karla F.C. *Passed On: African American Mourning Stories*. Durham and London: Duke University Press, 2002.

Hudson, Alfred Sereno. *The History of Sudbury, Massachusetts*. Sudbury, Mass., 1889.

Huff, Emma N., comp. *Memories That Live: Utah County Centennial History*. Springville, Utah: Art City Publishing Company, 1947.

Iwasaka, Michiko, and Barre Toelken. *Ghosts and the Japanese: Cultural Experience in Japanese Death Legends*. Logan: Utah State University Press, 1994.

Janvier, Thomas A. *Legends of the City of Mexico*. New York and London: Harper & Brothers. 1910, 162–65.

Johnson, Colleen Leahy. *Growing Up and Growing Old in Italian-American Families*. New Brunswick, N.J.: Rutgers University Press, 1985.

Jones, David. M. *Jazz Funeral: From the Inside*. (Film) New Orleans: DMJ Productions—WYES/TV, 1995.

Kalčik, Susan. "Ethnic Foodways in America: Symbol and the Performance of Identity." In *Ethnic and Regional Foodways in the United States: The Performance of Group Identity.* Linda Keller Brown and Kay Mussell, eds. Knoxville: University of Tennessee Press, 1997.

Karay, Mary Pyrros, and Fannie C. Nome, coeditors. *Hellenic Cuisine: A Collection of Greek Recipes.* Detroit, Mich.: St. Helen's Philoptochos Society and Sts. Constantine and Helen Parent-Teacher Association, 1985.

King, Julia A., and Douglas H. Ubelaker, eds. *Living and Dying on the 17th-Century Patuxent Frontier.* Crownsville, Md.: The Maryland Historical Trust Press, n.d.

Kinzie, Susan. "A Window into Memories: Auto Decals Gain in Popularity as a Way to Honor a Loved One." *Washington Post.* Saturday, August 28, 2004: Page B01.

Klein, Victor C. *New Orleans Ghosts.* Metairie, La.: Lycanthrope Press, 1996.

Kolatch, Alfred J. *The Jewish Mourner's Book of Why.* Middle Village, N.Y.: Jonathan David Publishers, Inc., 1996.

Kramer, Kenneth Paul. *The Sacred Art of Dying: How World Religions Understand Death.* New York/Mahwah: Paulist Press, 1988.

Kübler-Ross, Elisabeth. *On Death and Dying: What the Dying Have to Teach Doctors, Nurses, Clergy, and Their Own Families.* New York: Simon and Schuster (A Touchstone Book), 1969 (1997).

Kurlansky, Mark. *Salt: A World History.* New York: Penguin Books, Ltd., 2002.

Laderman, Gary. *Rest in Peace: A Cultural History of Death and the Funeral Business in Twentieth-Century America.* New York & Oxford: Oxford University Press, 2003.

———. *The Sacred Remains: American Attitudes toward Death, 1799–1883.* New Haven & London: Yale University Press, 1996.

Lamm, Maurice. *The Jewish Way of Death and Mourning.* Middle Village, N.Y.: Jonathan David Publishers, Inc., 2000.

Lattimore, Richmond. *The Iliad of Homer.* Chicago: The University of Chicago Press, 1961.

Lovric, Michelle. *Eccentric Epitaphs.* Oxford, England: Past Times Publishers, 2000a.

———. *Weird Wills & Eccentric Last Wishes.* Oxford, England: Past Times Publishers, 2000b.

Malloy, Thomas A., and Brenda Malloy. "The Disappearing Shaker Cemetery." In *Markers IX: The Journal of the Association for Gravestone Studies.* Theodore Chase, ed. Worcester, Mass.: Association for Gravestone Studies, 1992.

Malloy, Tom, and Brenda Malloy. "Gravemarkers and Memorials of King

Philip's War." In *Markers XXI: Annual Journal of the Association for Gravestone Studies.* Gary Collison, ed. Worcester, Mass.: Association for Gravestone Studies, 2004.

———. "Murder in Massachusetts: It's Written In Stone." *Markers XVI: Annual Journal of the Association for Gravestone Studies.* Richard E. Meyer, ed. Greenfield, Mass.: Association for Gravestone Studies, 1999.

Marsalis, Ellis L., Jr. *Rejoice When You Die: The New Orleans Jazz Funerals.* Baton Rouge: Louisiana State University Press, 1998.

McCarthy, Thomas C. "Hart Island." A presentation given as the American Culture Conference, November 7, 2004. Buffalo, New York.

McLuhan, Marshall. *Understanding Media: The Extensions of Man.* New York: Signet Books, 1964.

McMichael, George, gen. ed. *Anthology of American Literature, II. Realism to the Present.* 2nd Edition. New York: Macmillan Publishing Company, Inc., 1980.

Memorial Day. "The Origins of Memorial Day in the United States." <http://www.army.mil/cmh-pg/faq/memday/MD-Dev.htm>

Meyer, Richard E. "Pardon Me for Not Standing Up: Modern American Graveyard Humor." In *Of Corpse: Death and Humor in Folklore and Popular Culture,* ed. Peter Narváez. Logan: Utah State University Press, 2003.

Mickler, Ernest Matthew. *White Trash Cooking.* Berkeley, Calif.: Ten Speed Press, 1986.

Mintz, Sidney W. *Tasting Food, Tasting Freedom: Excursions into Eating, Culture, and the Past.* Boston, Mass.: Beacon Press, 1996.

Mitford, Jessica. *The American Way of Death.* Greenwich, Conn.: Fawcett Publications, 1963 (1983).

———. *The American Way of Death, Revisited.* New York: Alfred A. Knopf, 1998.

Moody, Raymond A. *Life After Life.* Toronto: Bantam Books, 1981.

Morreall, John. *Taking Laughter Seriously.* Albany: State University of New York Press, 1983.

Myerhoff, Barbara. *Number Our Days: A Triumph of Continuity and Culture among Jewish Old People in an Urban Ghetto.* New York: Simon and Schuster, 1980.

Narváez, Peter, ed. *Of Corpse: Death and Humor in Folklore and Popular Culture.* Logan: Utah State University Press, 2003.

National Council of Negro Women. *The Black Family Reunion Cookbook: Recipes and Memories.* New York: Fireside, 1993.

Noble, Allen G., and Ashok K. Dutt, eds. *India: Cultural Patterns and Processes.* Boulder, Co.: Westview Press, 1982.

Norrick, Neal R. *Conversational Joking: Humor in Everyday Talk*. Bloomington: Indiana University Press, 1993.

Olsen, Beth. Tape-recorded interview. July 29, 1997. Pleasant Grove, Utah.

Ortiz, Elisabeth Lambert. *The Complete Book of Mexican Cooking*. Philadelphia and New York: J.B. Lippincott Company, 1965.

O Súilleabháin, Seán. *Irish Wake Amusements*. Cork, Ireland: Mercier Press, 1967.

Paglia, Camille. "The Italian Way of Death." *Salon Premium*. August 4, 1996. <http://www.salon.com/weekly/paglia960805.html>

Patel, Lauri. Telephone Interview. Provo, Utah. February 9, 2004.

Patureau, Alan. "Catered Parties Replacing Post-Funeral Potlucks." *Atlanta Journal and Constitution*. June 20, 1995: D2.

Prothero, Stephen R. *Purified by Fire: A History of Cremation in America*. Berkeley: University of California Press, 2001.

Puckle, Bertram S. *Funeral Customs: Their Origin and Development*. London: T. Werner Laurie, 1926.

Pulcini, Robert, and Shari Springer Berman, directors. *The Young and the Dead*. HBO Video of Hollywood Forever Cemetery, 2003.

Raboteau, Albert J. *Slave Religion: The "Invisible Institution" in the Antebellum South*. Oxford/New York: Oxford University Press, 1980.

Ramsland, Katherine. *Cemetery Stories: Haunted Graveyards, Embalming Secrets, and the Life of a Corpse after Death*. New York: HarperCollins Publishers, Inc., 2001.

The Relief Society Action Manual. The Relief Society: Provo, Utah. Oak Hills Stake, 1996.

Robinson, Beverly. "Faith Is the Key and Prayer Unlocks the Door in African American Life." *Journal of American Folklore* Vol. 110, no. 438 (Fall 1997): 408–14.

Roden, Claudia. *The New Book of Middle Eastern Food*. New York: Alfred A. Knopf, 2001.

———. *The Book of Jewish Food: An Odyssey from Smarkand to New York*. New York: Alfred A. Knopf, 1999.

Rogak, Lisa. *Death Warmed Over: Funeral Food, Rituals, and Customs from around the World*. Berkeley and Toronto: Ten Speed Press, 2004.

Sacks, Daniel. *Whitebread Protestants: Food and Religion in American Culture*. New York: Palgrave, 2000.

Sargent, L.M. *Dealings with the Dead, by a Sexton of the Old School*. 2 vols. Boston: Dutton and Wentworth, 1856.

Saxon, Llyle, Edward Dreyer, and Robert Tallant. *Gumbo Ya-Ya: A Collection of Louisiana Folk Tales*. Gretna, La.: Pelican Publishing Company, 1998.

Shakespeare, William. *Much Ado about Nothing*. In *The Pelican Shakespeare*. Josephine Waters-Bennett, ed. New York: Penguin Books, 1971.

Siporin, Steve. American Studies 672: Jewish Folklife. Utah State University. Logan, Utah. January 9, 1990.

Smith, Jeff. *The Frugal Gourmet Cooks Three Ancient Cultures: China, Greece, Rome*. New York: William Morrow, 1989.

———. *The Frugal Gourmet on Our Immigrant Ancestors*. New York: Avon Books, 1990.

Spitzer, Nick. "Love and Death at the Second-Line." Unpublished Essay. Included with permission from the author. (February 2, 2004).

Steinbeck, John. *East of Eden*. New York: Penguin Group, 1992.

Steinberg, Milton. *Basic Judaism*. San Diego, New York, London: Harcourt Brace Jovanovich, 1975.

Sullivan, Lawrence E. *Native American Religions: North America: Religion, History, and Culture Selections from The Encyclopedia of Religion*, Mircea Eliade, editor-in-chief. New York: Macmillan Publishing Company, 1989.

Sully, James. *An Essay on Laughter: Its Forms, Its Causes, Its Development and Its Value*. London: Longmans Green, 1907.

Sutcher, Pam. Personal Interview. November 10, 2001. Provo, Utah.

Tannahill, Reay. *Food in History*. New York: Crown Publishers, Inc., 1989.

Thompson, Henry. "Cremation: Treatment of the Body after Death." *Contemporary Review* 23.2 (January 1874).

Thresholds Family Directed Funerals. <http://www.thresholds.us/index.asp>.

Tillich, Paul. *The Eternal Now*. London, England: SCM Press, 1963.

Toelken, Barre. "Dancing with the Departed: Japanese Obon in the American West." <http://www.worldandi.com/public/1994/c12/cfm>. 1994. Accessed June 21, 2005.

———. *The Dynamics of Folklore*. Logan: Utah State University Press, 1996.

———. Personal Interview. December 30, 2002. Logan, Utah.

Turner, Victor, ed. *Celebration: Studies in Festivity and Ritual*. Washington, D.C.: Smithsonian Institution Press, 1982.

Turner, Victor W. *The Ritual Process: Structure and Anti-Structure*. Chicago: Aldine Publishing Company, 1969.

Veblen, Thorstein. *The Theory of the Leisure Class*. New York: Viking Penguin, 1979.

Waugh, Evelyn. *The Loved One: An Anglo-American Tragedy*. Boston: Bay Back Books, Little, Brown and Company, (1948) 1999.

Weaver, William Woys. *America Eats: Forms of Edible Folk Art.* New York: Harper & Row, Publishers, Inc., (1899) 1989.

Webster's New World College Dictionary. Michael Agnes, ed. 4th edition. Cleveland, Ohio: Wiley Publishing, Inc., 2002.

Weinstein, Barry. Personal Interview. Baton Rouge, La. April 22, 2003.

What, Leslie. "Why We Wash the Dead: Caring for What Remains." *Parabola* Vol. 27, no. 2 (Summer 2002): 13–19.

Whiteley, Peter M. "The Southwest." In *Native American Religions North America: Religion, History, and Culture Selections from The Encyclopedia of Religion.* Lawrence E. Sullivan, ed. Mircea Eliade, editor-in-chief. New York: Macmillan Publishing Company, 1989.

<www.brainencyclopedia.com/encyclopedia/s/sp/space_burial.html>.

Young, Kristi. Personal Interview. January 24, 2004. Provo, Utah.

Zeitlin, Steve, and Ilana Harlow. *Giving Voice to Sorrow: Personal Responses to Death and Mourning.* New York: The Berkeley Publishing Group, 2001.

Index

5-13

DISCARD

CPSIA information can be obtained at www.ICGtesting.com
Printed in the USA
LVOW121325230413

330536LV00001B/62/P